CALLING THINGS

Amazing Miracles and Proof of Faith Testimonies!

CALLING THINGS...

Amazing Miracles and Proof of Faith Testimonies!

Denise D. Campbell

Calling Things
Amazing Miracles and Proof of Faith Testimonies

Authored and Published by Denise D. Campbell

Forward by Ce Ce Winans

Copyright © 2015 Denise D. Campbell

ISBN-13: 978-0692454022

ISBN-10: 0692454020

Printed in the United States of America.

Please note: Even though the testimonies in this book are all real... The names of the people have been changed to respect their privacy.

Unless otherwise stated all Scripture quotations come from the King James version of the Bible

www.ThePreferedBrand.com

DEDICATION

This book is dedicated to...

My relationship with my Senior Partner in life, the Holy Spirit; the Omnipotent, Omnipresent and Omniscient God! My spiritual evolution and the transformational journey that birthed the Holy Spirit encounters are reflected on these pages.

I am most grateful for the visionary insight of spiritual giants, (my Pastor; Dr. Bill Winston, Bishop David Oyedepo, Bishop Tudor Bismark, Bishop TD Jakes and Dr. Myles Munroe), that influenced me and my relationship with the Holy Spirit. Their passion for God, and dedication to delivering the Word through their teaching and writings, have provided me with an insatiable hunger and relentless pursuit of all that is Jesus Christ.

And to my Son, Ryan whose love and the promise of his Kingdom calling... sustained me throughout this life altering journey, filled with peaks and valleys and roads never traveled... until now... for such a time as this...

And to my dear friend, Shirley Strawberry, whose unconditional love, generosity and support never faltered in the best of times... and never... in the worst of times...

And to my friend, Sylvia Haygood for her loyalty, dependability and yes... her spiritual support and willingness to receive my Holy Spirit news... each and every time with genuine interest, excitement and encouragement.

And to my Sister, Debra Searles, for her persistent prayers, loyalty and friendship... unwavering in her faith that God would see me through... no matter what it looked like to the natural eye!

And to my niece, Missy Gaskin... always... and forever willing to be a help to me... to be the unpaid assistant... whether near or far... making no excuses... always coming through for me!

And to my friend, Brenda Jo Bowden for her graciousness, loving support.... And willingness to give me out of her want... for her editing expertise and the gift of her time... I truly thank God for her lifetime friendship...that transcends the miles...

And to my friend, Colette Blake Smith for her unselfish heart and spirit of purity... Her unconditional love and generosity renews in me the hope of love thy brother as thyself...

And to my Brother, Pastor Eric E. Jones, for his prayers and loving support throughout my lifetime.

A Special Dedication To: Stephen Alec Searles II

I would like to thank my nephew, Stephen Alec Searles II, for his loving support and ready ear, his receptive spirit... to always make the time to listen to my Holy Spirit stories; and the latest and greatest thing the Holy Spirit has done... I also want to thank Stephen for being the one that encouraged me to write this book. After having the willing heart to listen to the many miracles that were manifesting in my life; Stephen suggested to me, "Aunt Dee, you may want to begin to write these stories down... because they are going to continue to happen"... And even months later he asked me... if I had begun to record the miracles that were manifesting as he had suggested... I had to confess to him that I had not begun to write or commit them to paper...

Shortly thereafter, the Holy Spirit began to talk with me saying... "It is time to write the book of which I Star in the stories... You've been the vessel... but... I AM... the Star of these miracles, and these stories that demonstrate My Power... must be told!"

Stephen's unwavering faith in what God is doing in my life and the power of God to manifest miracles; positioned him to also become a recipient of the of Holy Spirit's outpouring of a miracle healing… the very morning he was scheduled for surgery! What had been there demanding in the natural to be surgically removed… miraculously disappeared by the power of God and unwavering faith! He truly became a witness to the miraculous!

Thanks Stephen for your loving spirit, patience to receive and listen to the long stories… and always an encouraging word for me as God has unfolded … miracle upon miracle in my life… Starring the Holy Spirit.

"Calling Things"… is definitely an outpouring of the Holy Spirit's gracious inspiration… encouraged by you!

A Special Dedication to the late Launa Thompson…

One of my life's most precious gifts; Launa Turner Thompson, was the epitome of a best friend. She gave me unconditional love, devotion and support. She championed my dreams and inspired my destiny. Launa encouraged me to always take time to *"Smell the Roses."*

While only hours before her transition, Launa took time to share her vision of my life's purpose and calling. She told me that God was calling for me to do some great things that I could never imagine, and that He was preparing me to soar! She asked me to find a church home for myself; one where I would be nurtured on His Word, in preparation for the calling God had on my life.

Launa wanted me to know for sure that she was going to be ok, and shared the following with me, in what ultimately was our last conversation.

After my commitment to her to find myself a church home; which satisfied her request... Launa then said to me... "Dee, I want you to know, I am at peace... and I am not afraid."

This life altering conversation with one of the finest women that has ever lived, led me down a road of destiny that orchestrated the foundation of my intimacy with God. My commitment to Launa to find myself a church home led me to place in Christ that I now surrender my all to Him.

Launa's abrupt and untimely death left a canyon size hole in the core of my life, yet the lessons she provided me, were clear examples of a lifestyle I can emulate; to always honor the standard of excellence that was her life.

Launa will forever occupy a seat on my "Personal Board of Directors." Thank you Launa, my "Cameo Queen," for the sacred connection that you and I will permanently share. Your memory transcends the passing of time because of the golden strands of love... you so graciously woven within my heart.

CONTENTS

ACKNOWLEDGEMENTS

I would like to acknowledge special family and friends that have supported, loved and prayed for me through this season... Thank you for your joyous response and encouragement... time and time again... to listen and receive with love... my encounters with the Holy Spirit!

Felice Searles, Theresa Smith, Dr. Katherine Washington, Dr. Andre Hines, Angela Winder, Tiffany Jordan, Darlene Morgan, Dorothy Thigpen, Ginnell Bunch, and Shirley Hogsett

FOREWORD

One of the greatest things to witness in a person's life is the transformation that comes from salvation! I have known Dee Dee Campbell for as long as I can remember. Dee Dee's mom and my mom have been the best of friends for years, and so our families... the Winans and the Joneses, grew up together. We lived in the Motor City; Detroit, Michigan and they lived in the Windy City; Chicago, Illinois. I can still remember the times they visited us and we visited them. It was always lots of laughter, lots of eating and lots of church!!

I have also, always admired Dee Dee's beauty! She could easily... still win a beauty contest today, but now I admire her inner beauty... far more than her outward beauty. To witness the transformation in her life because of salvation is nothing short of glorious! One conversation with Dee

Dee and you will know that she is completely in love with Jesus, and the Holy Spirit has become her closest friend.

Calling Things is a book full of incredible miracles and testimonies that are so encouraging to anyone who hears them. It's refreshing to know that The Holy Spirit is still moving miraculously in the lives of God's people. Dee Dee lives a life totally surrendered and dependent on God. Therefore, God is able to show Himself strong in her life and radically change the lives of others.

The Power of God's Word comes alive in Calling Things and I pray as you read it, the Power of God's Word will come alive in you! For God has not given us a spirit of fear but of power, and of love and of a sound mind. Calling Things reminds us there is nothing too hard for God... if you believe. Have faith in God and watch Him do the impossible for you, just like He did and continues to do for Dee Dee Campbell.

Go ahead... Call those things which be not as though they were, and watch and see what our amazing God will do for you.

I pray this book will take you to a place in God, you have never experienced before; a place where the impossible... is the norm!

- CeCe Winans

About CeCe Winans: If you ask CeCe Winans what drives her, the answer will be far removed from her endless list of accolades, best-selling albums, widespread industry recognition, and vast amounts of press coverage.

She'll make no mention of the multiple GRAMMY®, Stellar, and Dove awards she's garnered over the years, let alone the several gold-and platinum-certified albums she's scored-not even those she nabbed with brother BeBe as part of the hit-making duo BeBe & CeCe Winans.

She won't tell you she's graced the covers of high-profile publications such as Essence, Jet, CCM, and Today's Christian Woman, among countless others, or that she's made her rounds in the talk-show circuit, making appearances on The Today Show, Good Morning America, Oprah, Live with Regis & Kathie Lee, The Grammy's and more. And radio hits? Forget about it.

When all is said and done, CeCe's heart lies someplace else. Having recorded eight solo projects, she shares… " Whether you are sharing positive music, gospel, inspirational, or whatever you want to name it, you're teaching lessons to other people, which is still very important and nothing is more powerful than when you're face to face with God."

Much of CeCe's chart-topping music, has seen the singer entertaining her pop sensibilities, proving that she excels at interpreting buoyant, life-affirming songs that a wider audience could embrace. Not one to pick favorites, she says she loves both ends of the spectrum. But something about singing for God and His church strikes a cord in her that not even the most uplifting, stirring pop tune can. No matter where she stands in the musical spectrum, CeCe simply owns the lyric, cognizant that she's simply preparing the listener for deeper intimacy with the Divine God.

"It's great to sing songs that help us or that encourage us to live right, or to talk right, or to love each other-and those are all powerful messages, things that God smiles upon," CeCe says. "But when you just talk about the power of the living God and His awesomeness and His holiness, nothing is more powerful than that. It penetrates the heart more than anything."

INTRODUCTION

This heartfelt book was inspired by the amazing miracles and manifestations of the Holy Spirit in my life and throughout a journey... not of my choosing. I experienced and witnessed His miraculous glory and wonder, which I know without question were supernatural! I learned that these testimonies are *proof* that *God changes not!* His power for miracles, signs and wonders is clearly demonstrated and the stories that unfold... are *all* about Him!

My Senior Partner in life; The Omnipotent, The Omniscient and The Omnipresent, Holy Spirit is the *Star* of these stories, in which I am privileged to share His Magnificence... on the pages of this book. *All* testimonies point to Jesus, and I count it an unspeakable joy that He invited me into His adventures... I trust that my encounters, as I co-partnered with Him, will inspire and edify you, and that your faith will continuously elevate as a platform and as the currency to personally witness His undeniable power!

So What are Testimonies?

In the words of Bishop David O. Oyedepo:

"Testimonies are evidences of the faithfulness and integrity of God, the infallibility of Scriptures and the immutability of His counsel. They are triggers for victory in spiritual conflicts, as they energize the inner man for exploits!"

Testimonies are instruments of supernatural empowerment. They are the finger of God in action. They are as potent even when they happen to someone else because they have the power to reproduce themselves."

—Walking In The Miraculous

"For I Am the Lord, I change not;"

Malachi 3:6

"As it is written, I have made thee a father of many nations, before him whom he believed, even God, who quickeneth the dead, and calleth those things which be not as though they were."

- Romans 4:17

CHAPTER 1

A VISION OF DESTINY ON THE BEACH

Ten years ago, I had a dream...so I thought... It was as if I was awake while living out the unfolding of a very weird... but life-like episode of my life! Ten years later, I know with certainty that, that *"Dream"* was a *"Vision"* of my life that is purposely manifesting today.

Let me share this life altering preview into my future that is now...

It was the beginning of sunrise and the sky was completely dark; with the sun seeming to rest on top of the ocean. I was kneeling in the sand on the beach, in a state of meditation and prayer. As I looked up, across the sands from a distance, I could see my best friend Lisa walking toward me, hand in hand with a young woman. She approaches me and says, "Dee, will you help this young woman? She needs the blessing of your gifts."

I answered her by saying, "Sure Lisa," and then I asked the young woman to join me by saying, "Please kneel with me, pray with me." Lisa left only to return with a young man and another young woman, asking the same thing, "Dee, will you help these young people, they need the blessing of your gifts." I answered her in agreement of her request, asking the young people to join me in prayer. That scenario continued to happen as Lisa came and went, always returning with twice the number of people she had just deposited, requesting that I pray with them, for they were in need of the blessing of my gifts.

The bringing of people continued until there were more people surrounding me than the eyes could see or count. These people were diverse, and looked like a post card of *"we are the world."*

As I awakened from the "Dream," I realized two things were certain... *First-* that for the number of people that Lisa had brought, that now surrounds me as far as the eyes could see, I knew for sure that Lisa was *not* in the crowd and, *Second-* that when Lisa brought the people to me with whom I prayed, she never left any footprints …even in the sand!

When I was fully awake, I thought, "WOW! What was that?"

It was a dream that was alive, compelling and profound.

I phoned my friend, Lisa, and shared the dream with her. After hearing the dream, Lisa's immediate response was "Dee, we have to pray about that, it means something!"

I replied, "Lisa, you always want to pray about something, but all I know is that, after bringing all those people to me, asking me to help them... by repeatedly making that bizarre statement, 'Dee, will you help these people, they need the blessing of your gifts,' you didn't stay around to help!"

With that, she emphatically repeated, "Dee, we must pray about this... because it *does* mean something!"

Approximately three years later, in March 2004, Lisa organized a brainstorming session with people I trusted from my "inner circle" to come to my home as a strategy intervention for my career.

As my best friend, she did *not* check with me before planning this; she just called me up the morning of, and told me that they would be over at 5:00 pm. Lisa was doing this out of love and concern for me, and because she was convinced that God had me on a different path. She was confident that He had another *"Plan"* for my life.

Lisa was strongly persuaded that *His plan* did not include my present career path or the media industry, in which I'd invested the last decade of my life. The goal of the brainstorm was to ascertain a strategy to launch my speaking and leadership training into the marketplace. I wasn't exactly welcoming of this strategy to present my business ideas to this "inner circle." I really could not think of doing this training as a real career. It was something I was just doing as a *passion* on the side.

I never thought of it as a mission for my life or as part of a grand plan leading to the destiny to which God has purposed me.

I reluctantly shared my ideas with the "inner circle" that Lisa had assembled. The feedback was great and the validation that I definitely needed to take my training, leadership development and personal brand expertise, to the marketplace. At the conclusion of the brainstorm, Lisa looked at me and stated, "Dee, this is awesome! You must take your ideas to the marketplace!" She went on to confidently say, "Dee, I really think God wants you to do something else, and it doesn't include radio. I really feel He is calling you to do something new!"

Three months after the brainstorm, and three years after the "Dream", which I now know with certainty was a "Vision" of destiny; my friend, Lisa and I had another conversation.

It was June 19, 2004, and Lisa was critically ill and had spent the last week in the hospital. It was on a Saturday afternoon, and I was in Atlanta on business travel. Lisa was at home in Oak Park, having been released from the hospital on Friday evening.

As I was talking with her about her illness and our united fight ahead for her recovery… she silenced me by asking "Dee, will you do something for me?"

"Of course sweetie," was my reply.

Then I asked her, "What do you need?" Lisa asked me,

> "Dee, would you find yourself a church home, not like me, not like Nana, (the name she called my Mom), and not like Danielle, my sister, but a church home for you, where you can be nurtured and fed on God's Word.
>
> "You see Dee; you are getting ready to *soar* in God like never before! You are getting ready to do things that you could never have imagined doing. God is getting ready to launch you beyond your wildest dreams, and you are going to need the nurturing of a great church home, to prepare you, for what He has purposed you to do, in this earth!"

When I asked her how she knew these things of which she so confidently spoke of, Lisa replied… that she just did! As I repeatedly asked her, how she could possibly know these things, which she spoke of with such certainty, she remained calm and steadfast in her spirit, and answered in a quiet, yet unwavering conviction…

"I just do… You see Dee, God is going to use you in ways that you could never imagine and you are getting ready to *soar* in God like never before!"

And again she emphatically asked me, "Dee, will you do that for me, will you find yourself a great church home?" I answered her by committing to finding myself a great church home.

With my answer of yes, she went on to say a few other things that I also questioned her as to how she knew such things, speaking things as truth and reality, that had not taken place in my life, yet she spoke them as if she was reading my life's story... As if to *prophesy* of what was to come...

A story yet to unfold in the natural, as if she was *"Calling things that be not as though they were"*... *(Romans 4:17)*.

With every query from me, as I sought to hear logic and reasoning, she was consistent in replying that she knew ... just because she did.

Being satisfied with my commitment to finding myself a church home, Lisa ended our conversation by saying, "And Dee, I want you to know for sure, that I'm at peace and I'm not afraid!"

That was my last earthly conversation with my dearest friend.

Lisa transitioned early the next morning, on Father's Day... leaving a canyon size hole in my life, yet her unexpected death provided me with this priceless gift that chartered my quest... my journey; for not only a great church home, but my very own personal relationship with my heavenly Father.

It's been seven years since Lisa's death, and I'm in awe of the re-landscaping God has done with my life. I'm in awe of the manifestation of the "Vision of Destiny on The Beach!" I know for sure that I did not pick God; it was indeed He who picked me!

Everything that happened in the vision, specifically the praying for people, with a diversity of healing challenges, has manifested into miracle healings! The gift of healing continues to flow powerfully through me as a surrendered vessel of our Lord.

God has anointed me to use His virtue according to His will... to heal the sick; To stand on faith and witness miracles in the *right now*!

He has blessed and gifted me with this anointing. Lisa's statement in the vision of long ago, "Dee, these people need the blessing of your gifts"...is now my reality...in the natural.

> *"A Man's Gift will make room for him and bring him before great men." (Proverbs 18:16)*

Lisa's deathbed conversation and request of me to find myself a great church home, directed me to prepare for what God has called me to do, for such a time as this.

"To man belongs the plans of the heart, but from the Lord come the reply of the tongue."(Proverbs 16:1)

The "Vision of Destiny on the Beach," was a preview and description of the end of my life, not from the beginning.

Lisa's last request was to provide me with the tools of divine wisdom and revelation knowledge; to direct me for the course my journey was destined to take.

"In his heart a man plans his course, but the Lord determines his steps." (Proverbs 16:9)

"To man belongs The plans of the heart, But From the Lord Comes the reply Of the tongue."

- Proverbs 16:1

CHAPTER 2

THERE'S A LEADERSHIP MINISTRY ON YOUR LIFE!

In July of 2004, I was having drinks with my friend Judy, at the Drake Hotel in Chicago. Judy had invited me to join her while she waited to have dinner with Mrs. Dorothy Johnson and their Public Relations Director, later that evening. Judy and I were able to share a good part of the afternoon before her dinner guests arrived. The PR director, Linda, arrived first and joined us; as they now waited for the arrival of Mrs. Johnson.

We had an opportunity for great conversation and everyone appeared to enjoy the connection. It wasn't long before Mrs. Johnson arrived. Without prompting, I got up and went to bring her over to where we were sitting. I introduced myself and walked with her back to the group. We had small talk for just a short time before they concluded their visit with me; to head over to the restaurant for their dinner reservations.

The very next morning, I received a call from Judy. She asked me in a tone of wonderment; "Girl, what did you do to Mrs. Johnson?" I responded to her question by asking her, "What do you mean... what did I do to Mrs. Johnson. I was only with you for a short while of approximately fifteen to twenty minutes."

Judy went on to explain to me, what was prompting her questioning. She shared with me the conversation that Mrs. Johnson had initiated at dinner; with me as the subject.

Mrs. Johnson asked Judy a series of questions about me, which included, "Who is your friend, what is it that she does for a living, what is she doing now?"

When Judy wasn't giving her an answer that satisfied her reason for questioning; she continued to inquire, and then repeatedly made this statement...

"There is something about your friend...there is *something* about your friend!" She then told Judy that she wanted to meet me. When I asked Judy to give me more of an explanation of their conversation, she could only say that Mrs. Johnson seemed to be taken with me; to be in awe of me. She and their PR director could not understand what in the brief interaction with me, prior to dinner, had impacted or impressed Mrs. Johnson to the degree that she was obviously awed.

They did not understand what compelled her to spend so much of their evening inquiring about me, and continuously stating, "There is *something* about your friend!" Judy went on to say that perhaps Mrs. Johnson wanted to offer me an opportunity with the James Johnson Foundation... Some kind of job working with her at the organization...

Whatever was behind her asking to meet me... I was unquestionably happy to make that happen!

I was very excited to hear such wonderful and complimentary remarks about myself from such a dynamic and globally respected woman. Mrs. Johnson certainly had no hidden agenda or anything to personally gain from her comments of me; yet she felt compelled to meet me and wanted Judy to arrange the introduction. Judy told me that Mrs. Johnson wanted me to call her, so that we could set up a time for us to meet. "Oh Wow!"...was my response. This famous woman; mother of the world renowned NBA Champion, one of my heroes; Melvin Johnson... wanted to meet me?

I was too excited and couldn't wait to call her.

About two weeks later, Mrs. Johnson and I had lunch at the café in Neiman Marcus on the Gold Coast in Chicago; her suggestion for convenience. It was in the same building where her office for the James Johnson Foundation was located.

I had spent time leading up to our lunch, imagining what we'd share. I wondered what she would be like and continued to speculate why she wanted to meet *me*. I definitely was curious as to what prompted her to repeatedly say to Judy, *"There is something about your friend!"* I was really looking forward with anticipation and expectation... to our grand connection!

Our conversation at lunch flowed effortlessly. Mrs. Johnson's countenance and spirit created a space of ease and a level of comfort. Chatting with her was like talking with someone that you've known a long time. It was as if she knew me better than I knew myself.

I listened to her share her story, which reflected her life as a mother of a world famous legend, her career as a writer, and as a leader and role model. I shared my story with her, which included my life as a career woman in transition, and one who had just experienced the devastating loss of a best friend; just one month earlier. After two hours of sharing and getting to know one another, Mrs. Johnson became deliberate in spirit and began to speak; with purpose...

She looked up from her plate and said in a most serious tone, "Denise, I now know why I had to meet you... I don't know if Judy shared with you what I had told her about you. I said to Judy, there is something about your friend"... I did not know exactly what it was; but I knew it was *something...*

Mrs. Johnson went on to say "Now, I know what that something is, and it's what I saw that made me need to meet you!" She went on to say, "At first I thought there was something that I could have you do at the Foundation. But now having spent the last two hours with you; I now know that I could not ask you to do anything at the Foundation other than to lead it, if I were retiring!"

She went on to state, "I could not ask you to do anything in a follower's role. You have a *'Leadership Ministry'* on your life and it is like a bright light."

"You've been called to lead and therefore, you will *never,* ever have another follower's job in your life!"

She said that she could not tell me where to start; but she could advise me... "To just start where I am."

I was totally overwhelmed with Mrs. Johnson's revelation! It was intimidating and certainly not what I could have imagined she would say to me. In my wildest imagination, I would never have connected myself to the word, "Ministry"... of any sorts...

I knew in my spirit how incongruent this suggestion was to my present circumstances, my career and my lifestyle choices!

Why?

I wasn't even going to church on a regular basis, which was at the time, my only and very narrow perspective of one having a ministry...

Mrs. Johnson continued to share her thoughts on this compelling ministry calling on my life. From her perspective, she believed that she was spiritually selected to tell me what she'd been divinely given.

I left Mrs. Johnson that day; not knowing or possibly understanding the far reaching impact of what she had revealed to me, and how prophetic her revelation would be to my destiny!

In just a short time, opportunities to step out in Leadership roles began to appear! Opportunities to execute my leadership talent on a different platform; some that were not the result of my own efforts, began to *"seek"* me out.

I know now that they were divinely delivered to me as evidence of what Mrs. Johnson had spoken! Even so, I still wasn't able to wrap my brain around the idea of me having a *"Leadership Ministry"* or any ministry, for that matter!

After that prophetic conversation with Mrs. Johnson, my career pursuits extended to only leadership roles and contracts; working with businesses and their teams, and even life coaching other leaders in personal brand development. From that connection meeting with Mrs. Johnson, ten years ago to this day, I've not had another *"Follower's"* role...just as Mrs. Johnson had prophesied!

It certainly wasn't because I have not tried to get "regular" jobs that was commensurate with my talent and experience. That would have been a layup for me *before* the conversation. But, true to her prophesy, none of the opportunities that I've pursued, in less than a leader's role…have manifested.

I've applied for several positions whereas I thought it would surely happen…

After been interviewed and identified as a desired candidate, companies have flown me to New York, San Francisco, Miami, Tampa and Atlanta…only to have the jobs totally disappear…

To have that happen after several companies covered flight and hotel expenses, just never made any sense. Logic was completely out of the window!

I've learned from my journey over the last decade or so; the ministry that God has prepared me for…the Leadership Ministry of which Mrs. Johnson prophesied; don't make for logic or good sense…it is only making Faith!

The reality of my *now*, my Leadership Ministry… has been a process of connecting a lot of dots … a process of trusting what doesn't make sense and believing what my eyes cannot see…

As God continues to order my steps…I must believe that He chartered the course way back then to purposely position me at the Drake Hotel for a "coincidental" meeting with Mrs. Johnson, which has proven to be one that was… a *Divine Appointment*.

What He gave her to share with me was nothing short of divine! God amazes me on how He has and is continually re-landscaping my life!

As a man purposes in his heart, He orders their steps!

I'm totally *surrendered* today, after kicking and screaming for years, that God has *called* me to this Leadership Ministry-the Leadership Ministry that Mrs. Johnson so prophetically spoke of ten years ago.

I now embrace my powerful Kingdom assignment!   It was then and has always been God's irrevocable plan for my life!

> *"God, Who has saved us and called us with a Holy Calling, not according to our works, but according to His own purpose and grace which was given to us in Christ Jesus before time began." -II Timothy 1:9*

I welcome this special anointing that God has handpicked me to do in the earth as…

> *"I press toward the mark for the prize of the high calling of God in Christ Jesus," for such a time as this!" –Philippians 3:14.*

"A Man's gift will make room for him and bring him before great men."

- Proverbs 18:16

CHAPTER 3

GOD CAN MAKE MONEY
OUT OF SAND

It was July, 2009… I had been laid off from work for one year, and I was really experiencing some financial challenges. It was the first time ever that I was faced with the knowledge that I did not have a way to pay my mortgage. I tossed and turned most of the night, sleepless and worried over loss, and the lack of money. I finally got up and later that morning; while sitting at my desk, anxiety continued to rear its ugly voice, telling me that I didn't have any money to pay my mortgage, and all the terrible things that were going to happen to me. I fought back by *speaking the Word*, standing on scripture, Philippians 4:6, *"Be Anxious for Nothing but in all things by prayer and supplication with thanksgiving, make all your requests known to God."*

As the morning grew into the afternoon, I continued to meditate, repeat and speak this scripture. Later as I left home to run errands, I was driving in my car when the enemy started to torment me on my lack, and the "doom and gloom" of what would happen to me as a result of not paying my mortgage. Satan's presence filled my head as well as the car. It was as if he was sitting in the back seat; shouting at me...

I decided to speak the Word with authority and certainty, that what I was declaring is indeed true! I spoke Philippians 4:6, *"Be anxious for nothing but in all things by prayer and supplication, with thanksgiving, make all your requests known to God,"* and with that spoken Word, I hit the steering wheel of my car with the authority of my fist, and I made this decree: *"God can make money out of sand!"* Then I commanded the enemy to get out of my car!

And the Word tells me... *"Submit yourselves therefore to God. Resist the devil, and he will flee from you." - James 4:7*

That was approximately 1:00 in the afternoon. I completed my errands in peace and *without* any additional attacks from the enemy.

Later the same day, approximately 7:30 in the evening, I received a telephone call. It was from a new friend, someone who I'd known less than a year. This new acquaintance did not know the state of my financial status nor any of my personal information. We had not developed our relationship to the degree that she would know what I was going through. Even so, when I answered the phone, she asked me if I was okay. I told her yes, I was fine.

She asked me if I was sure, and I assured her again that I was fine. She then asked me if my son was okay. I told her he was fine too, healthy and standing in the need of prayer.

She probed a bit more, but eventually accepted that I was all right. I asked her why she was asking. She told me that I had been on her mind, constantly all day. She said that God would *not* allow her to stop thinking about me the entire day. She had not been able to call earlier, as her business responsibilities, kept her on conference calls and on appointments. This was her first opportunity to call me.

She then went on to say, "Denise, I don't know what is going on with you or your finances, but God spoke to me and told me to bring you $1000.00, and I was wondering if it would be acceptable for me to bring it to you?"

At that moment, something went through me… It had only been that very afternoon that I had decreed that "God can make money out of sand!" In less than seven hours, God had manifested not only $1000 out of nowhere (the unseen), but it was the exact amount that I needed to completely pay the mortgage!

It wasn't until later that God also brought to my remembrance, the Tithe that I'd paid in church on the previous Sunday. I had received an unemployment check of $420.00, so in obedience to my tithing commitment, I wrote a check for $42.00 and paid my tithe. Just days later, God supernaturally returned a Harvest of $1000.00-almost a 25 fold multiplier of my tithe of only $42.00!

The power of my decree in unwavering faith and my commitment to tithe, even in the face of natural lack, had produced a supernatural answer to my prayer *speedily*!

I walk in Spiritual Authority as a Believer, and with the certainty and dominion that God has given me as joint-heir with Jesus Christ... that my words... in faith produce what I decree...

> *Job 22:28, "And thou shall decree a thing and it shall be established unto thee!"*

> *Deuteronomy 8:18, "And you shall remember the Lord your God, for it is He who gives you power to get wealth, that He may establish His covenant which He swore to your fathers, as it is this day."*

Speak the Word and praise Him!

> *Matthew 9:29-30 "According to Your Faith, Be it Done Unto You!"*

"And you shall Remember The Lord your God, For it is He who gives you power to get wealth, That He may establish His covenant which He swore to your Fathers, As it is this day."

- Deuteronomy 8:18

Chapter 4

ACCESSING TOTAL RESTORATION BY FAITH; GOD'S MIRACLE ACCESSING TOOL!

In July of 2010, I received a call from my friend Linda. Linda was in a state of despair and in fear because of the news she'd just learned about her niece's, (Jackie), newborn son. Her niece was the love of her life and was the daughter she'd never had. She was feeling hopeless as how to help Jackie and her new born son in the face of the medical report just delivered by the doctors immediately after his birth. This infant was born with an urgent assault on his new life, because of an RH factor which was incompatible with his mother's blood and thus, poisonous to his own system.

Moments after his birth, he was put on life support and heart medication. He was in critical condition and began to experience seizures and consequently was put on antiseizure drugs as well. His prognosis for a normal life was dismal. He was placed on life support... Doctors told his Mom that he would never be normal; he would always be on medication, he would be challenged in the normal development of speaking, hearing and walking. They told her to expect developmental delays in his physical and intellectual capacity...

During the moments that Linda shared with me, the urgent condition of her niece's baby boy; God began to download in me just how to respond to her.

I stopped Linda by saying, "Wait a minute Linda, I am canceling that prognosis! Those doctors are not the final authority on Jackie's baby boy!" I began to decree, "In the name of Jesus, I am standing on scripture, Romans 4:17, *'Calling things that be not as though they were'* and I am believing in Faith that God is restoring his body, and he is healthy and completely restored... *Right Now!"*

I went on to decree and declare that not only will he *not* have to live on any medication, but I declared that he would be *totally* normal in his development. He would walk, talk and hear as if this episode of his young life... never took place. He would be developmentally normal with no effects from the present complications of his birth being evident! I informed Linda that the only thing required is our belief and unwavering Faith; regardless of the medical report and in the face of the current circumstances of him being in critical care. I boldly declared that God has totally healed and restored him!

As the days and weeks went into months...when I would inquire about Jackie's baby... Linda would say that the baby was getting better. I continued to believe God for total restoration and continued to be in Faith that manifestation in the *Natural* would come to reflect that which was already completed... *in the Supernatural*!

Linda and I had not talked much over the following year, and it had been quite a while since we had spoken, concerning the well-being and health of her great-nephew.

But on Saturday, June 25th, almost a year later, as I was talking with her, God dropped it in my spirit to ask Linda about him. I asked her to tell me how Jackie's little boy was doing...

She responded by telling me, "His development is totally normal and he is not on any medication! His doctors are completely perplexed about his healing and restoration; totally different from their prognosis a year ago!"

Praise God and give him all the Glory!

It was crucial that I ask Linda about her great-nephew; even a year later because God wanted me to see the power of His grace, and the workings of the Faith he extended to me to step out, and declare over the circumstances of Jackie's baby's complicated birth!

What the natural eye was limited to see and the imperfect reports of the doctors; would *not* dictate over God's plan for his normal life, and total restoration of health!

Hearing this miraculous news from Linda, continues to build my Faith in God's Word, and in the working of His mighty strength!

"According to Your Faith... Be it done unto you!"

"Be anxious for nothing But in all things by prayer And Supplication, With thanksgiving, Make all your requests Known to God."

- Philippians 4:6

CHAPTER 5

AUTHORITY OVER JAIL

The morning of August 28, 2011, my two sisters and I departed my home early, to travel to Indiana. We were going to visit my nephew, Caleb, who was incarcerated. It was to take us about four hours to get to the prison. My sister, Donna, Caleb's mom, had obtained directions from the correctional facility prior to our departure, and she was driving.

As we traveled, my two sisters and I were having a great time of connection. It was a beautiful day and the roads were clear. After we had traveled quite a distance; three hours plus, it appeared to us that we must be on the wrong road. We finally stopped a state trooper to ask for directions, and to our chagrin we had journeyed way out of the way. The directions that Donna was following, had taken us the opposite way from the prison. The trooper informed us that we were 150 miles off course, and so we were yet hours away... from our intended visit with Caleb. Looking at the clock and counting the distance, made the visit with Caleb seem unrealistic. In knowing this, my sister called ahead to the prison to alert them of our challenge. We had traveled for hours in the wrong direction and now we were heading there; albeit we would arrive very late, way past the scheduled hours for visitation.

She asked for special consideration, as she was from Charlotte, NC, and had not seen her son in a very long time. Donna was hoping the visit would be approved since we were so close. The prison guard listened, but her heart was hardened to Donna's story, and she told my sister that it was well beyond the time that we could be processed to see Caleb, so consequently, we would not be able to visit him. She further instructed Donna *not* to even come, for it would be a waste of time, because their rules would *not* allow for an exception to what she had spoken.

Donna got off the phone call and began to cry while sharing with us what the guard had said, relative to not even showing up. As she continued to cry, the Holy Spirit rose up in me and I said to her, "Stop crying... My Faith is at work... and it cannot work in an environment of worry and doubt!" She disagreed and told me that she could cry and still have Faith. Even so, I repeated my *position* for her to stop crying, because crying reflects that there is worry, and worry is only doubt... which symbolizes fear, and fear and faith cannot reside in the same space! With the Spiritual Authority in which the Holy Spirit was instructing me; I told her that we were going to see Caleb, and by faith it would happen... *if only we would believe!*

We were yet hours away from the prison, well beyond the 2:00 PM cut off for processing visitors to the prison.

We finally arrived at the prison. It was approximately 3:20 PM in natural time. As we approached the front of the prison, grounds' staff approached us and told us that we would not be able to see anyone due to the lateness of the hour. They told us that visiting hours had ended almost two hours ago. We listened and continued to approach the front of the prison to drop Donna off at the entrance, so that she could go on in, while we parked. My other sister Danielle and I parked the car, and went in to join Donna. When we got inside, Donna was leaning on the desk in obvious dismay, and tearfully said to us, "They are refusing to allow us to visit, and they are very upset with us for ignoring their order *not* to come at all!"

She pointed to the clock, saying that their clock seemed to be even later than what we thought the actual time was. It was showing about 4:00 PM, two hours past the time of processing and they reiterated that *no* exceptions would be made.

I asked Donna if she had requested to speak to someone that could make an exception... considering the circumstances of our long travel of seven hours, not to mention the broken heart of a mother attempting to visit her son. My sister replied that she had made that appeal, even so, the only woman guard behind the desk had told her *no*!

With that answer, the Holy Spirit began down loading directions to me; speaking clearly to me...

I approached the same woman guard and asked her if I could speak with her. She looked up and I quietly asked her, "Is there someone you could call on our behalf? This visit is so important to my sister."

She looked at me and gently answered saying, "Yes there was someone; her supervisor." I then asked her if she would please call her supervisor for us. She looked at me while the other five or six guards looked on, and answered me with a calm yes. She said, "Yes I will call him for you."

She instructed us to go and have a seat, and that she would call her supervisor right away. My sisters and I went to be seated and waited to speak with the guard's supervisor.

Shortly thereafter, her supervisor came out and approached us...

On approaching us, he commented that he had been informed of our story, and that as sympathetic as he was to our circumstances, there was still nothing that he could do for us. He simply reiterated what we had already been told, "We have our rules and the rules cannot be changed no matter what the situation might be."

I listened to him speaking to us and as I tuned inward to pay attention... to hear from my spirit, *The Holy Spirit* began to instruct me on what to say next.

After the supervisor had finished with his reasoning on why he must also refuse our request, I then said to him,

"I understand that you have rules and the time is late; even so I peacefully and respectfully ask you, is there anyone you could call that could say yes to our visiting Caleb, and if so, who would you have to call?" He looked at me as if never telling his narrative of *"no"*... and said yes! "Well, yes, ma'am. Yes, I can call my own supervisor."

I looked at him and asked him then, would he call his superior for us; one who could enable our visit with Caleb. He responded with, "Yes, yes he would call him and asked us to wait."

We continued to sit and wait until another officer showed up. This officer asked us who was the mother and who were we trying to visit. My sister Donna spoke up and identified herself as the inmate's mother, and told him that his name is Caleb. He then said to her as we listened, that he could not bend the rules for us or anyone. He told us, "The prisoners have been put down for the evening, and exceptions to the rule were not to be extended for anyone. To his chagrin, he also must say *no* to our request to visit with Caleb."

Again I listened for the Holy Spirit to give me directions of my next step. *By now*, I'm confident in my spiritual authority as a believer. As the Holy Spirit directed me, I asked this now *third* guard if there was someone he could call that could possibly say yes and allow us this exception. After asking, I just remained quiet... yet continued to look directly at him, while waiting for his response. Moments passed when he, like the other two guards before him, didn't know why... *after saying no...* ended up saying yes.

He said, "Well, yes there is someone he could call that could say yes to your request." Again, with a calm humbleness, I asked him if he would call his superior for us so that my sisters and I could visit my nephew. Without reservation, he replied that he would make that call!

As we waited for now the *fourth* guard; a higher authority within the prison system, to come speak with us, the Holy Spirit continued to confirm His presence within me. His persuasive voice continued to strengthen me in His power, might and authority!

The fourth guard came out to speak with us, and quickly told us that he had heard our story... Even so, the rules for the prison must stand and *not* be broken under any circumstance. He let us know that he had heard a variety of reasons as to why people are late for prisoners' visits, and he simply could not be responsible for people not being able to follow directions, that make them miss the regulated visiting hours. He said to us that he must say *no* to our request for this visit.

By now, I am directly speaking with the confidence and authority delegated to me by the Holy Spirit! Listening for that still small voice; being downloaded with additional instructions on what to say *yet* to this persistent no, and refusal from the prison authorities to allow our visit.

Once again, I looked at this guard, and tell him I do understand... what he just said to us, and that I realize that they have rules, by which they govern the correctional facility.

With that being said, I gently asked him the same question that the Holy Spirit had given to me to ask the very first guard at the desk...

I asked him if there was a person that he could call that had the authority to say yes to our dilemma, and that would allow us this visit with Caleb, and if so, who would that be. A moment or two passed by and he answered me with a confirming yes. Yes, there is a higher up that he could call that could make our visit possible. I then asked him if he would do that, would he make that call for us. His reply was yes and he asked us to wait while he went to make that call.

Minutes later, a now *fifth* guard came out to speak with us. This guard had ocean blue eyes and very white blond hair. I believe he was the captain or the highest ranking official of the prison on duty that day. He came over to us and reviewed what he had been told of our plight. He let us know that he had heard so many stories of why people did not arrive in the hours set aside for visitation, and that most of those he did *not* believe!

He told us again that the rules for the prison could not be broken for any circumstance. At this time, being unwavering in faith... I just started speaking as the Holy Spirit began taking over...*again*...

I asked him the very same question yet again. Was there someone he could call that would allow us to see Caleb ... today? He stared at me with his piercing blue eyes and moments later, his no became a yes! He said he would make a call!

He went through a door and just minutes later, came right back and said this to us...

He told us that he had good news and bad news for us...

First the good news...

For as much as he heard many stories and had not believed them, for *some reason* he was going to allow us a visit with Caleb! The bad news he said was that he could only allow us to visit him for just one hour!

Hallelujah! My sisters and I began to rejoice right there! Praise God! The Holy Spirit had prevailed and faith was *unlocking the doors to the prison gates!* The Holy Spirit had given me step by step instructions on how to walk out my delegated Authority as a believer. This was definitely a testimony of faith over trials, and spiritual authority triumphing... after a multitude of *"No's!"*

Praise God, for my sisters and I... staying in faith, in the face of what our eyes could see and what our ears were hearing. I know for sure that the power of the Holy Spirit was flowing, and that my sisters witnessed the supernatural working, on our behalf!

Even the prison guards and my nephew, Caleb, could not believe what had just taken place! We were allowed access and were able to visit Caleb... who was completely in disbelief that the prison allowed a visit this late; well beyond regulated visiting hours!

This certainly was the manifestation of the sons of God; inside the prison gates! And just like Apostle Paul and Silas... the locks on the prison gates...opened...for us!

> *"And at midnight Paul and Silas prayed, and sang praises unto God: and the prisoners heard them. And suddenly there was a great earthquake, so that the foundations of the prison were shaken: and immediately all the doors were opened, and every one's bands were loosed." –Acts 16:22-26*

Thank you Holy Spirit for showing up in the power of your might, and for allowing me to walk in the Authority of the

Righteous! I am the righteousness of God and the seed of the righteous shall be delivered!

Praise God for empowering me to stand in unwavering faith, and always causing me to triumph!

"Now thanks be unto God which always causeth us to triumph in Christ, And maketh manifest the savour of His knowledge by us in every place."

- 2 Corinthians 2:14

CHAPTER 6

I DECREE TOTAL RESTORATION FOR YOUR SISTER

One morning while I was substitute teaching in a local high school, I received a telephone call from a good friend. Under normal circumstances, I would not have even answered the phone because I was in a classroom; instructing students, and had put my phone on vibrate. I had just dismissed the first period class and my phone began vibrating, on the desk where it was laying. I looked at caller ID and recognized that my friend Evelyn was calling, and decided to take her call.

Evelyn began the conversation by saying, "Denise, I need you to do two things for me. First I need to ask you to pray for my sister."

On saying that, her voice cracked, and she began to cry. She went on to say, "Denise, I thought that I had lost my sister the other day. You see, I had not heard from her, nor could I get in touch with her by phone, and no one in the family had been in contact with her."

She went on to say, "I was so concerned because my sister is very sick and has been on the waiting list for a liver transplant for over four years. I was so worried when she did not answer that I had the police to do a welfare check. They broke into her home and found her lying in her own soil and unconscious! She was rushed to the hospital and is now in critical care."

Evelyn went on to share, "Denise, I asked God who could pray for my sister this morning and he gave me you. Denise, I've *watched* your life, and I know how you live, so I know you can pray for my sister... Denise, will you pray for my sister?"

Inasmuch as she was asking me to pray for her sister, she meant... would I pray later.

I responded to her, saying... "We are going to pray for your sister Right Now!" With faith as my access key, I began to pray and speak out to God saying... "I am calling for total and complete restoration of your sister's health! I am standing on scripture; the unwavering Word of God, Romans: 4:17 *'Calling things that be not as though they were.'*

When I finished praying, I told Evelyn, "I'm believing in faith that your sister's healing is done *right now!* It is already done! We are not looking to the present circumstances or listening to what the doctors are saying. We are believing for complete restoration of her health and nothing less! I am decreeing these things are already done in Jesus' name, Amen!"

After finishing the prayer for her sister, Evelyn continued talking with me about the second thing she wanted to ask me.

While we were talking, her call waiting clicked in, and she said to me, "Denise, hold on... That is the hospital trying to reach me, I have to take it, but please don't go anywhere... I need to finish talking with you... Please wait."

As God would have it, I was still in the classroom alone, as no students had arrived for the second period, and neither had the teacher returned whose class I was covering. Finally she resumed our call with an elevated excitement and exclaimed,

"Denise, Denise! While you were praying, while you were on the phone with me praying, a compatible liver for my sister has come through! The surgeons are prepping her for surgery *right now!*"

In amazement to what she was saying, I asked, "What... Wait a minute...how long has your sister been on the liver transplant waiting list?" She replied, "She's been on the waiting list... over four years!" She then told me she needed to go, but she would call me back.

When she called me later that same afternoon, she told me that the doctors said that this was nothing short of a *miracle*!

They explained to Evelyn,

"In urgent cases like her sister, even *if* a compatible organ shows up—due to how critically ill she has become—in most cases, she would be ineligible for the transplant, and would *not* be given the organ!"

God moved speedily in that moment of prayer, accessing His favor...standing firmly in faith!

People are waiting for the manifestation of the Sons of God! In less than twenty-four hours, Evelyn's sister, received her new liver, and within a week... was released from the hospital. A couple months later, at the time of sharing this testimony with my church body, she was living her life with renewed vigor, and as if she never had been critically ill!

"According to Your Faith, Be it done unto you!"

"And thou shall Decree a thing and it shall be established unto thee!"

- *Job 22:28*

CHAPTER 7

ACCESSING THE MIRACLE POWER OF GOD BY FAITH LORETTA'S UNCLE - PART 1

I am particularly excited to share this faith testimony with you!

I am in awe of God's Mighty Hand! In April, my friend Loretta called me with a heavy heart. She shared with me the story of her uncle; her Father's last sibling and the devastating news he'd received from his doctors. His prognosis was dismal at best. He, already being a dialysis patient, was diagnosed with lung cancer which had metastasized throughout his body. His diagnosis also revealed cancer, now in his kidney, prostate and a bone in his leg. He, who had lost a lot of weight, was in the hospital being prepped for surgery.

My friend shared with me her Father's sadness on this life ending news about his brother, and that he had been crying all week in despair. As I listened to my friend, God dropped in on me and I asked her if her uncle had Faith. She replied that she really didn't know. She thought he probably went to church sometimes, and that she thought he believed in God, but she wasn't sure *if he had any Faith...*

I responded by telling her, "Well, now would be an excellent time to start having faith!" I said to her, "I am going to pray for your uncle and in faith; I am accessing the Healing Power of God Almighty. And I am absolutely standing on Romans 4:17, *Calling things that be not as though they were!"* I let my friend know that I was calling for her uncle's complete restoration, and in the Name of Jesus; I am declaring that he is 100% restored!

I told her to get off the phone with me, and instructed her to call her Dad and Mom. I told her to inform them of the victorious news of her uncle's compete healing and restoration. I advised her to instruct them *not* to look at the doctors' reports and to *not* look at his present circumstances. Regardless of what is being said of his condition in the moment, I told them that their loved one is completely restored by faith, and that we are looking for the manifestation of that decree... and nothing less!

A couple of weeks passed by and I had not heard from Loretta. One night, God nudged me out of my sleep and told me to call her, to get the *Victory* news about her uncle! It was passed 11:00 at night and I knew my friend to be well asleep by that hour, but in obedience to my God; I texted her.

I wrote:

"Hey, call me and tell me the *Victory News* of your uncle's restoration." I didn't hear back for a couple of days. When she did respond, she then wrote,

"The really great news is that his lung biopsy came back---*NO CANCER!!!! Praise GOD!!* We passed the first test, more blessing to follow! Thanks for your prayers."

I wrote back..."There is no First Test! It is already done... *ALL* of it!

My God is a complete healer that does not need to do just a little at a time... even so; He requires Complete and *UNWAVERING FAITH*...

I continued to respond to her text by saying:

"As I prayed, I stood in the gap for nothing less than complete restoration, and MY GOD has delivered JUST that... It is already done! Praise Him right now for Complete Victory! We are not waiting on what the doctors would say... We walk by faith, not by sight! I told her that I'd *called* for your Uncle's Healing and Restoration *before* the biopsy reports... that's the Power of Faith that releases God's Unmerited Grace!"

After that night... time passed and having not heard anything back from Loretta since that day... The Holy Spirit directed me to call her, two months later... and I asked her, "Tell me the Victory News of your Uncle's Restoration." She responded by telling me, *"All his Cancer is gone!"* She told me that after the lung biopsy was negative, the doctors were in disbelief and perplexed for this man had shown evidence of cancer throughout his lungs and other areas of his body during previous tests. In their certainty of being right about their medical diagnosis; they performed a more intrusive exam to ascertain his cancer status. When that procedure was completed and the results were read...

It was without a doubt.... *NO CANCER*... Anywhere in his Body! They could only respond with...

"We cannot figure out what has happened... he is no longer showing the Cancer that was previously there!"

The doctors merely speculated that this was some kind of a *miracle*, but I know for certain it was a *miracle* performed only by the mighty power of God, and through prayer; accessing His Grace by Unwavering Faith! I Praise Him and give God all the Glory! Cause not by me, lest I would boast... but by His grace and the power of the faith, in which He is forever renewing in me; God has made Loretta's Uncle...whole!

> *"Then Jesus answered and said to her, 'O woman, great is your faith! Let it be to you as you desire.' And her daughter was healed from that very hour."*
> *–Matthew 15:28*

"According to to your Faith be it done unto you."

- Matthew 9:29-30

CHAPTER 8

ACCESSING THE MIRACLE POWER OF GOD BY FAITH LORETTA'S UNCLE - PART 2

I am overjoyed to share this testimony of faith with you, which continues the unwavering manifestation of God's glory and its miracle-producing power!

Three months ago, I shared a testimony of a miracle healing whereas my friend's uncle had been completely restored from cancer. The prognosis received from his doctors was bleak. He, already being a dialysis patient, was diagnosed with lung cancer which had metastasized throughout his body with cancer now in his kidney, prostate and a bone in his leg. He went through surgery, and all areas in suspect... were found to be cancer-free, which totally perplexed the medical team reviewing his results.

Last month, two months since his miracle healing and after a declaration of total victory; my friend shared with me that her uncle is sick again! His doctors were telling him that he had cancer again, and that he needed to begin radiation right away in the next week!

I was mystified! I asked, "Which uncle?" I was unconvinced! I said to my friend, "You're telling me the same uncle who was healed, now has cancer again?"

"Yes, Denise! We don't have a lot of information about it yet, but he is very sick again." She stated. Even as I remembered that God clearly told me that He would restore my friend's uncle and I surely believed that... I have to say my faith was *challenged* by the news.

That night as I prayed, I cried out to God, and asked him the same thing that Moses asked him while on Mount Sinai, "What have I left undone? You told me that Loretta's Uncle was totally restored so he *cannot* have cancer!"

On the following Sunday, during service, the news of Loretta's uncle continued to challenge my faith and even so, I continued to decree, "In the name of Jesus... He does *not* have cancer!"

I continued to stand on scripture, Romans 4:17, *"Calling things that be not as though they were."*

Monday came with me standing *firm and unwavering* on that Word! On Tuesday morning, I called Loretta, leaving her a message, declaring that her uncle did *not* have cancer and asking her to call me so that we could call her uncle together. I wanted to pray directly with him! I did not hear from her until two days later, onThursday morning.

When I answered the phone, she was sobbing and saying to me, "Denise, I need you to pray...pray hard Denise, pray hard!"

She anxiously exclaimed, "My friend Russell; Dina's husband is in a coma." Loretta then said to me, that she needed to go into a meeting at that moment, so she would call me back...

That night, after not hearing from Loretta all day, even after a couple of phone calls, Satan attempted to tell me that it had become a worse situation, which was the reasoning behind Loretta not calling back.

So, I texted her scripture which confessed my faith that restoration for Russell was done and completely so! I pressed into God's Word and one of my favorite Scriptures...

> *John 14:12, "Verily, verily, I say unto you, that He that believeth on Me, the works that I do shall he do also; and greater works than these shall he do; because I go to my Father."*

It wasn't until Friday evening that Loretta finally called. She said to me,

"Denise, it's a *miracle!* After getting to the hospital this morning, I walked into Russell's room and he has completely come out of the coma." She went on to share that Dina stated, her husband had died; that he had flat lined on the table! Now looking at him, she begin to shout, "It's a miracle that he is restored, and is now talking with us!"

Loretta said to me, "I am calling you to acknowledge prayer!" What she shared next was astonishing even to me!

"Denise, I went to my Mother's house this evening. Upon entering, my mother asked me to guess who was in her kitchen. I said, "It can't be Uncle Russell!" She responded, "That's exactly who it is!" Loretta greeted her uncle excitedly and asked him "How are you able to be up and around after having just started radiation for the latest diagnosis of cancer?"

Her uncle responded by saying, "Loretta, those people don't know what they are talking about! *They could not do the radiation because they could not find the cancer!"* He proclaimed, "Loretta, I do *not* have cancer!"

Loretta said to me, "Denise this is two miracles showing up on the same day and I wanted to acknowledge the power of prayer! These things are nothing short of *miracles!"* I told Loretta, "It is all God and none of me! I glorify His awesome power and exalt His name on High!"

Loretta then said to me, "Denise, you were so certain that my uncle did not have cancer! I got all your phone messages on Tuesday, stating you wanted to pray directly with my uncle because you were certain... he did not have cancer, and *Now*...the doctors are saying what you already knew!"

Praise God for unwavering Faith, even in the face of conflicting reports and circumstances! I'm determined to believe the report of the Lord!

Isaiah 55:1 tells us, *"Who hath believed our report? and to whom is the arm of the Lord revealed?"*

"Then Jesus answered and said to her, 'O woman, great is your faith! Let it be to you as you desire.' And her daughter was healed from that very hour."

- Matthew 15:28

CHAPTER 9

FLOWING IN THE SUPERNATURAL! FAITH... THE ACCESS TOOL TO VICTORY OVER COMA

God's supernatural anointing is flowing in the miraculous! Let me share a story of God's wondrous power to heal when hope in the natural evades the senses.

Last Sunday, I was visiting a family member's home for dinner and shortly after arriving; our cousin Ricky comes downstairs in a hurried state. He shared a story of despair, telling us he'd just learned of a childhood friend's critical health. His friend had been severely injured in an attack and was now in a coma. He was in angst and was on his way to the hospital, having just spoken to his friend's brother. He stated that his friend was going to die, and he was rushing to the hospital to see him. Ricky anxiously gathered his belongings, and I could see the fear in his face as he was preparing to leave...

I called out to him and asked him to wait a minute. The Holy Spirit had downloaded in me to tell him with unwavering certainty ...that his friend did not have to die! I asked him his friend's name. He said that his friend's name was Derrick. I asked him if I could pray with him for his friend's healing before he left for the hospital. Ricky agreed to the prayer, so I joined hands with him and two other family members that were there. I began the prayer by saying, "Lord, I boldly approach the throne of grace and as I am standing in unwavering Faith on the scripture; Romans 4:17, I am *"Calling things that be not as though they were."*

I was calling for complete restoration of Derrick's health and decreeing that his healing was complete from the crown of his head to the soles of his feet! When I finished praying; I told Ricky to go to the hospital in faith. I told him when he got there, to *expect a change...*

I asked him to call me back with an update on Derrick's restoration and healing. After about two hours, I had not heard from him so I checked with others to see if he had phoned them. He had not. The evening ended without me receiving any word from Ricky. The next day, my phone rang with caller ID revealing that Ricky was calling. Upon answering, Ricky was calling; inquiring about missing keys from yesterday's dinner, even so, I had an opportunity to ask him about Derrick. He said that Derrick was doing *much better*, but he needed to go...

About an hour later, God dropped it in my spirit to call Ricky back and question him about Derrick. I called him back and asked him to tell me again what he had shared on yesterday, when he declared that Derrick was getting ready to die. He reminded me that he shared with us that Derrick was in a coma and he was informed by Derrick's brother, that he was probably going to die.

With that being said, I then asked him, what he meant by saying that Derrick was now *"much better"*...

He told me that when he arrived in Derrick's hospital room, he who had been in a coma... *opened* his eyes a couple of times... a sign of hope and definitely an improvement over... "He's getting ready to die!"

The week went by and on Saturday morning... six days later, I received a phone call from Ricky; saying "I am calling to thank you for your prayers...   As we speak, my friend Derrick is sitting up, and beginning to talk!"

Derrick had come completely out of his coma!   I began to praise the Lord for this miraculous victory!

Only six days before, Ricky was in angst and heartbroken *and* stating that his friend was getting ready to die.   Now, he was acknowledging the miracle-working power of the Almighty God that had restored his friend; bringing him out of the clenches of death ...restoring him from a state of coma!

When I asked Ricky what the Doctors were saying, he shared with me that on Sunday, they had given Derrick only a 30% chance of living. He had undergone a craniotomy; which is brain surgery to remove a bone from his skull, thus reducing the pressure in his head resulting from the severe injury he'd sustained from an assault. And today, supernatural victory had been granted by God that offers us hope when in the natural... there is none!

God is so worthy to be praised! I continue to praise Him for flowing supernaturally through my life and for the *privilege* to be a vessel... for His healing virtue! None of this is by me...lest I would boast ...but by the Grace of God that He chooses to use the faith of a believer... Jesus said that believers would do the things that He did, and greater works would they do! I *choose* to take Him at His Word!

> *"Verily, verily, I say unto you, He that believeth on Me, the works that I do shall he do also; and greater works than these shall he do; because I go to my Father." - John 14:12*

The world is waiting on the manifestation of the Sons of God!

> *"According to Your Faith...Be it Done Unto You!" - Matthew 9:29-30*

"Verily, Verily, I say unto you, he that believeth on me, the works that I do shall he do also; and greater works than thse shall he do; because I go unto my Father."

- John 14:12

CHAPTER 10

GOD'S MIRACLE POWER TO HEAL KIDNEYS... AND REVERSE HIGH BLOOD PRESSURE!

I received a phone call on October 12, 2011, from my niece by marriage, Francis, who lives in Sacramento, California. She told me she wanted to share a testimony with me. With that being said, I became very excited and told her to share it with me. She went on to inquire of me, if I remembered when she had asked me to pray for her sister that lives in Chicago. I did not at first, so I asked her to refresh my memory... She reminded me that it had been some time ago, maybe three to four months. At the time she asked for prayer, I had recently released my testimony of God's miracle healing power! It revealed God's amazing power to intervene in our lives, as I shared the story of my friend's sister. After a prayer of faith, she miraculously received a new liver after being on the transplant waiting list for over four years! Upon hearing that testimony that yielded proof of God's miracle working power when accessed by faith, Francis took a step of faith to call; believing if God did it for someone else... He would do it for her sister!

Francis called and asked me to pray for her sister, Tasha, who was a kidney dialysis patient and also waiting on the transplant list for a kidney. I agreed to pray for her sister and asked her to do a three-way connection by adding her sister to the call. Unbeknownst to me, Tasha was currently going to dialysis three times each week. I prayed for her sister, calling for her complete restoration, standing on my anchor scripture of Romans 4:17, *"Call things that be not, as though they were."* I instructed Tasha to stay in unwavering Faith for her complete healing and total restoration, for she was completely restored from the crown of her head to the soles of her feet! I directed her to continue to say, *"By His Stripes I am Healed!"*

My niece admitted that she had not really talked with her sister since the prayer, even so, she would check on how she was doing through her conversations with her Mom. Francis informed me that Tasha was previously scheduled for surgery to receive a kidney transplant. Unfortunately for Tanya, just before the transplant was to take place, the family withdrew her from being the recipient; designating the organ to go to someone else, along with all the other organs. The family decided to provide them to only one recipient. Being very disappointed, Tasha had to continue her three times weekly dialysis appointments, as she went back on the kidney transplant waiting list.

So here is Tasha's testimony:

My niece, Francis, received a call from her sister earlier today and this is what she shared:

During one of Tasha's dialysis treatments, her doctor notified her that he wanted her to come in to his office, because he needed to talk with her. Initially, she was alarmed that her doctor was requesting to see her, even so, she set up the appointment to follow up with him. At her visit with her doctor, He told her he had some news to share with her, but first wanted to ask her if she was doing something *different.* Tasha replied no, telling him that she was not doing anything different. She confirmed that she had not changed her routine, diet or anything. Her doctor informed her that he had good news about her kidneys. He went on to say, *"It seems that your kidneys have healed themselves! All your levels have returned to normal, to the levels of healthy kidneys!"*

He continued to share with Tasha, that the possibility of what has happened to her was extremely rare; and that the chance of this happening to kidneys which had been in the failing state; the condition that hers were in, would only be 10%! He actually told her that this is a *miracle*!

Her doctor told her that he would be watching her, but would most likely be taking her off of dialysis!

In addition to the miraculous healing concerning her kidneys, Tasha had more *miracle* news to share of God's restoration power! She went on to share with us that she had been challenged with hypertension, and had been on medication for it, the last six years. With the restoration and the healing of her kidneys, an added benefit of God's miracle working power had *also* healed her from high blood pressure! She informed me that her high blood pressure was completely reversed and her blood pressure was now perfectly normal! Tasha brought to my remembrance as she recalled what I'd spoken to her during the prayer. Tasha told me what I had said while praying for her. I prayed, "Everything that is not in agreement with your total restoration will come in line! From the top of your head to the soles of your feet, I decree you are healed!" And *without* Tasha making any changes in her diet and food selections, her blood pressure reverted to normal! Total reversal by the power of God! Her normal blood pressure compelled her doctors to take her completely off all medicine for Hypertension!

Tasha, along with her doctors embrace this total healing as a miracle from God and acknowledge, *Prayer and Faith* as the difference maker in her life and restoration!

I give God all the glory for His supernatural manifestation for such a time as this! I am in awe of His miracle working power, and I'm humbled that He has supernaturally engrafted me to serve as a vessel in His Kingdom!

I stand on John 14:12, *"Very truly I tell you, whoever believes in me will do the works I have been doing, and they will do even greater things than these, because I am going to the Father."*

I celebrate and revere His awesome power and Give Him all the glory! I am in His service!

"Do you not believe that I am in the Father, and the Father in me? The words that I speak to you I do not speak on My own authority; but the Father who dwells in Me does the works. Believe me that I am in the Father and the Father in Me, or else believe Me for the sake of the works themselves."

- John 14:10-11

CHAPTER 11

GOUT BOWS DOWN TO FAITH!

In the summer of 2011, I called to check on my Aunt Bell, my Mom's last living sibling. I make an effort to connect with her from time to time just to make sure that she is doing well. When speaking with her that day, and asking her how she was feeling, she began to tell me of her painful challenge with Gout. She told me that she had been experiencing symptoms of leg and ankle swelling, painful tenderness and inflammation of her foot. The condition had lasted for over two weeks. When she finished describing her ailment and the pain that was persisting, I was moved in my spirit to pray a prayer of faith with her. I asked her if her Pastor had prayed for her. She replied yes that he had. As she was answering me, Satan attempted to discourage me from praying by whispering in my ear, "Now, you don't think that you can pray better than her Pastor?" And as quickly as Satan whispered his statement, God spoke to me in His irresistible voice, "It is not the better prayer...it is the prayers of the righteous that availeth much... plural!"

God spoke directly to me to pray for her and confirmed to me, that praying for her, showed no disrespect to her Pastor's prayer. So I said to Aunt Bell, "I am going to pray a prayer of faith for you, and all I need for you to do, is to believe that God would heal you, and for you to stay in unwavering faith that you are completely restored!" She agreed that she wanted the prayer, and with that, I prayed. I stood on the power of the Word, Romans 4:17, *"Calling things that be not as though they were,"* and proclaimed her complete healing and restoration! Standing on Job 22:28, *"And thou shall decree a thing and it shall be establish unto thee, and light will shine upon your ways,"* I decreed that her gout would disappear and that all her swelling in her foot, ankle and leg would be gone!

When I finished praying for my aunt, I made this declaration of faith! I told her with the spiritual authority given to me... *that by this time tomorrow,* she would call me proclaiming victory over Gout! I said to her, "You will no longer have Gout, that all your pain will be gone, and that all of the swelling will have disappeared!" So I asked Aunt Bell to call me the next day... and that I would be *expecting* a call...that proclaimed her restoration and her victory over Gout!

Approximately twenty four hours later, my phone rang and the caller ID indicated that it was my Aunt Bell calling.

Even though I was in a grocery store, I was certain of the victory! I answered the call standing in the middle of the produce department! I greeted my Aunt with, "OK Aunt Bell, tell me the victory report!"

Aunt Bell answered me by saying, "Dee, my leg and ankle is no longer swollen and all my pain is gone!" Praise the Lord! I begin to give God thanks for His healing power and the power of faith to restore! My Aunt Bell concluded by saying to me, "Dee, you can always pray for me... anytime!" Faith demanded that Gout must flee...and it fled!

I am in awe of God's wondrous power, and how every impossibility... is at the mercy of faith! He has anointed me to heal...and I exercise my Spiritual Authority by *"Calling things that be not as though they were!"* – Romans 4:17

I know that it is the power of God working through me to perform miracles today. God is the same yesterday, today and forever! He is the Lord and changes not!

I firmly believe, and stand in agreement with what Jesus told His disciples in John 14:12, *"Verily, verily, I say unto you, if thou can believe in me, the works that I do you will do also, and greater works than these will you do, because I go to my Father."*

I believe... I receive... and I possess! I am taking God at His Word! I am agreeing with the Word of God!

Our Heavenly Father has empowered us as partakers of the *New Covenant,* with the ability to perform miracles as

Ambassadors of the Kingdom! I am so honored to represent His Kingdom on earth! Praise His glorious name!

"He who has My commandments and keeps them, it is he who loves Me. And he who loves Me will be loved by My Father, and I will love him and manifest Myself to him."

- John 14:21

CHAPTER 12

WALKING RESTORED SUPERNATURALLY!

Early during the summer of 2011, I took a ride with my dear friend and church buddy Sonya, as she needed to go visit the Mother of her recently deceased friend. I really was going for the purposes of her needing me to navigate the south side of Chicago which was unfamiliar territory to her. We arrived and went into the home of Mrs. Wilkins and upon entering; she introduced us to her friend who was sitting on the sofa.

After a few minutes, Mrs. Wilkins left the room and went to another part of the house. While we were waiting for her to return, her friend on the sofa began to speak to us. Without any prompting or apparent reason, she began to share with us, her story of disability. She told us that she was really in a lot of pain with her leg and in her back, and she was very challenged and limited in her ability to get around even with her cane, which lay on the floor beside her. As I did not know her or even her name at the moment, I was just listening to her share her sad story...

Without any notice, Sonya begins to respond to the woman...

Sonya said to the woman, "Well, would you like Denise to pray for you? She's been anointed to heal and she can pray for your healing"... With that being said, the woman responded by saying, "Yes, I'd like her to pray for me." It took me a moment to realize... that they were talking about me!

I reacted by getting up off the couch where I'd been sitting next to Sonya, and asking the woman, Mrs. Henry, if she could stand with me as I pray. She was able to stand, and as I reached out to hold her hand, I asked Sonya to join us. Right there, in the middle of Mrs. Wilkins' living room... the three of us went into prayer as I stood on God's infallible Word, Romans 4:17, *"Calling things that be not as though they were."* I called for her total restoration and healing. In faith, and in the name of Jesus, I decreed her pain was gone and that she was restored!

While I was yet praying, I could feel a sudden jerky movement from Mrs. Henry, as I held her hands. As soon as I finished praying, Mrs. Henry asked me in an elevated voice, "What was that *thing* that went up and down my leg and across my back...and down my leg again?" I looked at her, not responding right away, but moments later, the *Spirit of God* gave me this to ask her. I said to her, "Well, do you feel better?" She answered yes that she did feel better... even so; she wanted me to tell her what was that feeling that had gone through her body that made her jerk... I went on to tell her, that the movement she felt that ran up and down her leg, and through her back, was probably the Holy Spirit... releasing the pain in her body.

As I was sharing the *Holy Spirit's* explanation with her, Mrs. Wilkins; overhearing her friend's elevated voice, came back in and asked, "Did I miss something?" Mrs. Henry responded to her by answering, "Yes! When Denise; meaning me, prayed for me, something went up and down my leg and across my back and down my leg again!"

On hearing this, Mrs. Wilkins looked at me and asked, "Well, will you pray for me? I have Melanoma and I would like you to pray for me." I agreed that I would pray for her as well. As I begin to engage all of us, by holding hands, Mrs. Wilkins' adult son and adult grandson came from the back of the house saying, that they wanted prayer too... and joined the circle of prayer. As we began, another guest came from the back of the house after overhearing us, and also stated, she too wanted to have prayer.

So there, in the middle of Mrs. Wilkins' home, I prayed for all those who were requesting prayer. I stood unwavering on the power of God's incorruptible Word that fails not! I prayed Romans 4:17, *"Calling things that be not as though they were."* I finished praying for the group and shortly thereafter Sonya and I departed the home.

Approximately one week later, I got a call from Sonya. Sonya sounded very excited when I answered the phone, and begin to share with me the manifestation of God's miracle working power!

She told me that Mrs. Wilkins had phoned her earlier that day. She explained to Sonya that she had received a call from Mrs. Henry's daughter, who wanted to get my telephone number. She wanted to call me and ask me, "What happened with her Mother last week?" "What happened in that house?" She went on to tell Mrs. Wilkins that her Mom, since that prayer...was *now* doing things... that she had *not* done or been able to do... in years! Mrs. Henry was walking around, going to and from, and having full use of her legs. By faith, God had truly restored her ability to walk!

I, along with Sonya, began to rejoice and praise God for His Faithfulness! God is so awesome! He is performing miracles today through His anointed ambassadors of the Kingdom! I'm honored that He has appointed me for such a time as this; as Men are waiting for the manifestations of the Sons of God! Christianity was never meant to be dictated; it was always meant to be demonstrated! It is my privilege to serve the Lord as He directs my path! Praise His majestic name!

"Insomuch that the multitude wondered, when they saw the dumb to speak, the maimed to be whole, and the lame to walk, and the blind to see: and they glorified the God of Israel."

- Matthew 15:31

CHAPTER 13

MY ENCOUNTER WITH THE SUPERNATURAL!

Earlier this year, on the morning of July 11, 2011, I was preparing to have my morning devotion. As I gathered all that I needed before sitting down, I placed a bottle of water on the table where I would be studying. As I placed the water on the table, I noticed something that was silver laying close to my Bible and devotional reading materials. I instinctively picked it up and realized it was a ring. I immediately thought, "Um... where did this come from?" Not recognizing it, and being focused on beginning my devotion, I moved to set the ring back where I'd found it. As I did so, a glimpse of something written on the ring caught my eye. The inscription on the ring was too small for my naked eye to read so I picked up my reading glasses. On top of the ring was written, *"Purity"* and inside the ring was the word, *"Forgiven."* I then again wondered and voiced out loud, "Where did this come from...how did this ring get here?" I knew that I had not brought the ring into my home. I knew that no one else had bought it for me; neither had I had any visitors that could have placed it there! So I placed it back on the table without knowing or getting an answer, and finished collecting all that I needed to start, and I began my devotion…

I was reading a book written by Bishop David Oyedepo. As I read, I was cross referencing the scriptures utilized in reading the book's passages. At one point the book's scriptural reference sent me to *Acts 10:38*. As I turned my Bible pages to go to that scripture, The Holy Spirit downloaded in my spirit, to *re-read* the overview of the book of Acts. The reason that I say re-read, is because I'd already read the overview which was previously highlighted. At first, I resisted the instruction to re-read it, rationalizing to the great Omniscient Holy Spirit… that I had already read it… and in response to my rationalization, He sternly repeated… *"Re-read it!"*

At His admonishment… and now in obedience to the voice of God to read it, I turned to the overview to read it again. I begin to read the Introduction to Acts which talked about how God empowers men and women who stand for Him, with the Holy Spirit. It goes on to explain that God fills ordinary people with His Spirit and commission them to influence the world. Miracles occur as God confirms His Word with signs, wonders and miracles following. The overview continued to say that God is looking for His leaders and the Church to be established in *"Purity"* so that He could empower it without limits…

He entrusts His power to the "Pure" and this overview in Acts… specifically notes the sequence as; first *"Purity,"* then "Power," then "Proclamation," and finally "Penetration!"

As I finished the reading of the overview, I was totally in awe of the many references to *"Purity,"* just thirty minutes after discovering the *"Purity"* ring amongst my devotional materials! In amazement, I picked up the *"Purity"* ring once again and questioned its appearance by asking out loud, "God, where did this ring come from, how did it get here?" Immediately, I got an answer!

What sounded like the audible voice of God filling my living room… began to speak to my spirit saying…

"Daughter, you've been flowing in the supernatural and when I arrive for a visit, don't question my arrival!"

The voice of God filled my spirit with such certainty; that without question or any doubt… I knew for sure with unwavering conviction that the *"Purity"* ring had manifested from the supernatural! I indeed was walking in the *4th dimension*; operating in the miraculous… where the Almighty Creator… creates!

From that moment on… I've not questioned the origin of the ring and know with resolute faith, that surely I had *"An Encounter with The Supernatural!"*

At the time of the discovery of the ring, I did not realize the significance of *"Purity"* as an irrevocable requirement, for those who are committed to God's vision of impacting the world for Christ! As explained by Bishop Oyedepo,

"Purity is what gives you access to the instructions of wisdom and leads to your distinction on the earth!" – Bishop David Oyedepo-*"The Wisdom That Works"*

When reflecting on the sequence of the non-negotiable leadership qualities which God is commanding of his leaders...

I looked inside my own life...

First, Purity... I received the *"Purity"* ring; supernaturally!

Second, Power; The Power of The Supernatural; The Holy Spirit, has flowed through me... manifesting numerous miracles.

Third, Proclamation; I gave a testimony of a liver transplant and the miracle therein, proclaiming God's supernatural manifestation by faith, after which... a surge of miracles has followed and continue to manifest!

Lastly, Penetration... my testimony of the liver transplant miracle was recorded and went forth...globally during the International Faith Conference! Technology provided our connection to over one hundred and thirty nations! My Faith has gone global! *WOW!*

What a way to penetrate and to provide answers to the groans of the people of the world, who are waiting on the "Manifestation of the Sons of God!"

In faith, I'm totally surrendered to stay purified as a vessel where His virtue can flow! Yielding my will to His, I'm agreeing with His Word and walking worthy of His anointing to carry out my Kingdom assignment. I am humbled by the many blessings of the Holy Spirit gifts, and by my encounter with the Supernatural, as evidenced by His delivery of my very own *"Purity"* ring... delivered... "supernaturally!"

"How God anointed Jesus of Nazareth with the Holy Ghost and with power: who went about doing good, and healing all that were oppressed of the devil; for God was with him."

- Acts 10:38

"Jesus answered and said unto him, If a man love me, he will keep my words: and my Father will love him, and we will come unto him, and make our abode with him."

- John 14:23

CHAPTER 14

FAITH IS A BLANK CHECK...
IF YOU WILL BELIEVE!

On the morning of February 7, 2012, Tresse, (who's like a daughter to me/she is mother of my granddaughter, Reagan), dressed Reagan and dropped her off at school. She returned home and started to prepare for her work day. She had been home only a short time when she lost consciousness, and was found by a friend in her home. Finding her unresponsive, he promptly called the paramedics to her home. When they attempted to revive Tresse, they quickly discovered that she did not have a pulse nor did she have a heartbeat... They moved speedily to treat her by cutting away her clothing and using a difibulator to restart her heart. Then snatching her up, without waiting on a stretcher; carried her to the ambulance and on to the hospital.

I begin to receive urgent text messages as I sat miles away at a conference. I could see the red light blinking on my silenced phone; communicating to my spirit that I should take a look. As I picked up the phone, I read the several messages which were all urgent; stating emergency... *"Tresse at hospital, please call!"* The messages were from Gerri, Tresse's aunt. My natural responses wanted to panic as I stood to leave the auditorium. As I navigated myself through the conference crowd, the Holy Spirit began to speak to me, reminding me of God's Word. I begin to speak Philippians 4:6, *"Be anxious for nothing but in all things by prayer and supplication, with thanksgiving, make all your requests known to God."* The calm of God's infallible Word came over me as I walked out of the convention hall where I could get a signal. I phoned Gerri who answered right away; recapping the morning's unfortunate circumstances, and sharing with me the devastating news of Tresse's sudden illness.

Tresse was in urgent care and had been put into a medically induced coma. She was on a breathing machine and was hooked up to multiple IV's and monitors. At this point, the doctors were trying to ascertain what prompted Tresse's heart to completely stop. They did not have a clue and were not ruling out anything including stroke, aneurism, heart attack or blood clot.

I said to Gerri that I wanted to pray right now for Tresse's total restoration and by faith I was *"Calling things that be not as though they were" (Romans 4:17).* I told her not to look at the circumstances but to stay in faith that God has restored Tresse already, and that she was totally healed. I asked her to keep meditating and staying in faith by saying, *"By His stripes, she is healed!"*

Being away at the conference, I wasn't able to get to Tresse on that day. By evening the doctors wanted her to rest and not have any additional visitors, while they continued to test and guess... about her medical condition, its cause and ultimately their prognosis.

The next day, I met several members of Tresse's family at the hospital where they shared yesterday's events of her trauma. People came and went throughout the day as the news spread of her illness. She was yet on a respirator and still in an induced coma. The doctors ordered multiple body scans of major organs; trying as best as they could to determine what happened. They were completely at a loss in identifying exact reasons or any medical rationale as to what could have occurred, to make the heart of a seemingly healthy thirty-three year old woman... *just stop*!

After being at the hospital for several hours, I initiated prayer with family members as we encircled the unconscious Tresse, lying on her hospital bed. I told them not to look at the many machines that were monitoring Tresse's condition. I encouraged them to stay in unshakeable faith for Tresse's total restoration, and to believe with me that God had already healed her completely! Before I left the hospital for the day, I told Tresse's brother; Darren... that Tresse was completely healed and reminded him of the miracle that God had performed for his friend last summer, as we prayed in Gerri's kitchen. I asked him not to look at the machines or the current circumstances that we could see with our eyes, but to stay in faith... for she was completely restored! I told him, "When it was all said and done, the medical team will use the word *"Miracle"*...to describe Tresse's healing!"

With that, I left for home; being that it was the first day of our Winter Faith Refresher at Living Word Christian Center! I couldn't wait to get to service, for I know that a refreshing of faith for such a time as this... was in perfect time!

I came in at the end of "Corporate Prayer," and when it was asked if anyone needed special prayer, I raised my hand. As the saints encircled me in prayer and asked me of my need, I told them this... "I have just left Loyola Hospital where Tresse, who is the mother of my granddaughter, and like my own daughter, lies in a critical state." I quickly recapped the events of her sudden illness. With that being said, I told them, that I had *already prayed* for her total restoration, standing on scripture, Romans 4:17, *"Calling things that be not as though they were,"* and by faith I was confident that Tresse had been restored! I shared with them that I had told her brother that God had performed a *Miracle* in Tresse's body, and that the medical team would use the word *Miracle*...to describe Tresse's healing, when all was said and done! My prayer request of them, was to *"stand in agreement"* with me! Standing on the Word of God, the saints prayed the prayer of agreement with me.

> *"Again I say unto you, That if two of you shall agree on earth as touching anything that they shall ask, it shall be done for them of my Father which is in heaven." –Matthew 18:19*

That first night of the winter faith refresher was powerful! Pastor Bill Winston was on fire! In his sermon, Pastor used an analogy that really struck home with me. He said that faith is a "Blank Check"... ready to be used by us at any time! He said that we could write it out for whatever we choose! The idea of faith being a "Blank Check" that could be cashed at my covenant bank account... powerfully intrigued me!

As service ended for the night; being full of the Holy Spirit from the powerful message and the anointing of Pastor's sermon, I headed for my car. Though the hour was late, I felt led by the Spirit to go back to the hospital to visit with Tresse. I called ahead to speak with Gerri... hoping to get an update on how she was doing. When talking with Gerri and asking her for a status update on tests taken that day, she really didn't have any new information on test results. She told me that the results were not back and still the doctors did not know what had prompt her heart to stop. But the Holy Spirit quickened me to ask her, "What are they *saying* about her status, what are they *saying* about her medically; even without test results?" Gerri responded and said to me, "They said it is simply a *miracle!*"

I begin to rejoice at the awesome power of God and His miraculous healing power! It was on the very day that I declared in faith to Darren; her brother, that they would use the word *Miracle*...and only hours later... before the day ended...they did! Praise God's Holy name and the power of His prayer of agreement!

After leaving the hospital at midnight, I got home and remembered that my nephew Sean was due to have a biopsy in the morning. I wanted to have prayer with Sean who was in Sacramento, California, and with his mom, my sister, who lives in Charlotte, NC. By this time it was 1:00 AM in Charlotte and 10:00 pm in Sacramento. I didn't think about time and I considered not the hour! I was moving in the Spirit to call... so I did. I got my sister Danielle on the line first and told her I wanted to pray for Sean's biopsy, so I was going to do a three way call. Together we called and prayed for him. I told Sean that I was standing on Romans 4:17; *"Calling things that be not as though they were!"* I informed Sean that I had a word from the Holy Spirit for him and that he should only be expecting a good report in the morning! And by faith that is all he should expect!

We got off the call and the power of Pastor's sermon continued to speak to me. It's now about 1:00 AM, and I remembered the analogy of the "Blank Check." I pulled out a new journal and decided that I would use that analogy to write out a check against my heavenly bank account.

I wrote out three things that I wanted to cash in faith! The first was Tresse's total restoration, second was Sean's good report and third, Martha's complete deliverance. (Martha is another relative of mine that I'd been interceding for in prayer for her healing; which was being challenged with a medical report indicating a mass in her kidney)

The next morning after dressing and heading to the hospital to visit with Tresse, the Holy Spirit prompted me to call and check in on Sean. As soon as the Holy Spirit spoke to me, Satan spoke up and said to me, it was too early to call Sean as it was only 9:00 AM in California, and he had only gone to surgery at 8 o'clock. I told Satan to shut up and that I was going to call him now!

I phoned his wife Fatima as I knew he could be in surgery. When Fatima answered, I asked her about the process and what were the doctors *saying...* She told me that the doctors were not saying anything yet, and that nothing was going on. I continued to press her to tell me what were the doctors saying, even if they were not doing anything as of yet... She answered me saying, "Surgery has been delayed due to the fact that the doctors could not find the growth, so they have been unable to proceed with Sean's surgery!" I quickly began to give God praise for what I knew for certain; that Sean had received his healing through the miraculous removal of the suspicious growth.

I began to rejoice and I told Fatima... that they could not find it because I had decreed it would only be a good report! She attempted to calm my excited rejoicing of God's miracle working power in operation! She quickly explained that the team of the three doctors were in disbelief as to where it could have gone... And that they moved to order a CAT scan to fully uncover what was going on with Sean. With the confidence I have in God... I declared to her, "It doesn't matter what test they order; the *mass will not be found;* for Sean was completely healed and miraculously restored!"

After the CAT scan, Sean's results were the same... the mass was gone! God's miracles cannot be explained! *He is...and it is so!*

A little while later, I arrived at the hospital to see Tresse. I was still on a *spiritual high* from the awesome news of Sean's miracle, and last night's news of Tresse from the medical team...being spoken of as... *"She's just a miracle!"*

Tresse condition continued to improve that day with her being removed from the breathing machine and slowly coming to awareness that she was in the hospital. By Friday, the 4th day since becoming ill, one of the doctors shared an update with Gerri and me. He told us that the teams of physicians were yet trying to ascertain her condition and prognosis; even so, they had not been able to provide a definitive medical explanation. With that being said, I *asked* him once again how they would describe her status. He looked directly at me and answered... *"She is just a miracle, it's just a miracle!"*

Tresse's condition was indeed a medical mystery to them. I knew for certain, it was a miracle of God's limitless power to heal! Tresse received a miracle of complete restoration that left no clues as to what happened. God's complete miracle-working power restored to the original state, leaving no evidence of any illness!

Over the next few days, the medical doctors continued to share their best guess work with us, asking if this had happened to anyone else in the family. By the weekend, Tresse was removed from urgent care to another room. Still without an exact explanation as to what led her to this *"medical mystery,"* she continued to improve as her doctors would communicate; even so, they could not explain a cause...

Without being able to pinpoint a medical cause that makes logic, the doctors shifted gears on what to say about Tresse. After days of tests and no real answers, the medical team focused on prevention for the future; installing a defibrillator in Tresse's chest. They summarized the cause for the interruption of her heartbeat as something in her DNA and/or genetics...

Years later... Tresse continues to walk in the miracle of her restoration! I give God all the praise and glory; for nothing is too hard for God! He sent His Word and it healed her!

"And being not weak in faith, [I considered not Tresse's condition or the unexplainable circumstances of her illness...] I staggered not at the promise of God through unbelief; but being strong in faith, giving glory to God; and being fully persuaded that... what He had promised, He was able to perform." –Romans 4:19-21

"Therefore I say unto you, Whatsoever things you ask when you pray, Believe that you receive them, and You will have them."

- Mark 11:24

CHAPTER 15

FAITH CONQUERS
BLOOD CANCER!

Monday morning on February 29th, Marvis, my workout partner and I, were at the health club preparing to begin our exercise routine. She was having a conversation with a woman of Asian descent as I was waiting for her. I waited as she finished talking and then we headed toward the stairs. Marvis begins to share with me news about the woman, with whom she'd been talking. As we climbed the stairs, she told me that this woman had blood cancer and has to have monthly blood transfusions. I felt the normal compassion for her... but in a split second; the Holy Spirit began to speak to me. He clearly instructed me to pray for that woman and He told me, she would be made whole! I spoke up to Marvis and said to her, "Marvis, I need to pray for that woman!"

She replied by saying to me that we could pray for her when we went back downstairs. I agreed with her and began my workout. While going through my exercise regimen, the Holy Spirit would not let my spirit rest. He continued to speak to me about praying for the Asian woman; telling me the prayer would make her whole. I tried to ignore the inner voice which was speaking to me with such clarity. After a while, I could not resist the still small voice of the Holy Spirit, so I went back over to Marvis and told her that I *must* pray for the woman, and shared with her that the Holy Spirit was clearly telling me so! She agreed, so we finished up and went downstairs. We looked all around the locker room and could not find her. It quickly became apparent that she had left. I was really disappointed that I'd missed her; even more so, that I had not obeyed the specific instructions of the Holy Spirit to pray for her.

On Tuesday, the very next day as I went about my schedule, the Holy Spirit continued to speak with me concerning the woman from the health club. He repeatedly told me that I should have prayed for her; for she would be made whole. The next morning which was Wednesday, as I prepared to go to the gym, the still small voice of the Holy Spirit spoke to me yet again about praying for the woman with the blood cancer. When Marvis arrived to pick me up, I got in the car and shared with her the incessant promptings of the Holy Spirit, saying that I must pray for the woman that morning when we arrive at the club. Upon entering the locker room, Marvis and I searched for the Asian woman.

At first it did not appear that she was there, but as we continued to look for her she came around from the other side of the lockers and began to speak to Marvis. I stood close by as she was talking with Marvis; sharing with her the update of a recent blood transfusion to battle the cancer. As they were talking, the Holy Spirit begins to whisper to me. The Holy Spirit revealed to me, that Marvis; although being a born again believer… was uncomfortable about introducing me to this woman, and telling her that I wanted to pray for her. He said to me that I would have to speak up and tell the woman myself! I softly put my hand on her shoulder and looked at her, asking if it would be alright if I prayed for her. She looked back at me and told me *No!* She said to me that she didn't need me to pray for her because she prayed for herself. She said that praying for herself made her happy, so she did it all the time and she really did not need me to pray for her. As I looked on, she continued to share with Marvis the detailed news about her health and wellness regime.

Meanwhile, I continued to rest my hand on her shoulder, ever so gently and with the patience of the Holy Spirit. After a short time had passed, she quit talking and looked up at me, being tiny in stature; she said to me, *"Yes, you can pray for me!"* Her no had suddenly *…turned to yes!* "Yes, you can pray for me" She said!

I ushered her out of the aisle; moving to an area where I could pray. I introduced myself and she told me that her name was Nancy. I began praying for Nancy, a prayer of faith; standing on scripture, Romans 4:17, *"Calling things that be not as though they were."* As I finished the prayer, I told her that God *had* restored her and stated that she no longer had blood cancer! I shared Isaiah 53:5 with her and encouraged her to continually meditate on it, saying out loud... *"By His stripes I am healed."* I reminded Nancy not to consider the doctors' reports or the physical circumstances of her illness, but to stay in unwavering faith that God had delivered her totally from blood cancer, and to *expect* complete restoration from her illness!

Nancy shared with me that she had never learned to read the Bible, and asked me if I could send her the scriptures that I just prayed for her. I told her that I could do it right now. Last year, the Holy Spirit instructed me to start keeping scriptures in my Blackberry. I begin to compose an arsenal of God's Word for such a time as this, although at the time; not knowing that I would be using it for purposes of my Kingdom assignment. So, I got Nancy's number and right there on the spot I was able to send her the prayer for Divine Healing! I wished her well and reminded her to stay in faith and to continually meditate God's Word, day and night!

On March 6th, almost a week later, specifically six days, I began to hear from the Spirit. I had not seen Nancy since the day of praying for her in the locker room. The Holy Spirit begin to speak to me concerning people that I'd recently prayed for, and instructed me to send them some additional faith inspired reminders; encouraging them to stay committed to their healing by speaking words of faith. I compiled a list of folks which included Nancy, and sent out God's Word on healing by faith, emphasizing in my text that The Word is an all purpose drug for divine health!

About an hour later, I received a response by text from Nancy. This is what she said to me...

> *"I see changes in my body! My dark gray skin is now back to its natural color, my blackened foot is now close to natural and I feel the Lord! I thank you for all the blessing coming my way. I adore your love and kindness."*

I responded to Nancy's text by telling her... to continue to proclaim His divine healing in her body and to keep saying, *"By His stripes I am healed!"* She responded to me stating that she would keep saying, *"By His stripes I am healed!"*

Oh what an awesome God we serve! What a miracle of divine restoration!

I continue to be in reverence of God's almighty power that He works through me as a yielded and surrendered vessel. I stand in faith knowing that it is *God that does the work!*

Remembering what Jesus shared with the disciples, I too am walking in my Kingdom assignment!

> *"Do you not believe that I am in the Father, and the Father in Me? The words that I speak to you I do not speak on My own authority; but the Father who*

dwells in Me does the works. Believe me that I am in the Father and the Father in Me, or else believe Me for the sake of the works themselves. Verily, verily, I say unto you, He that believeth on Me, the works that I do shall he do also; and greater works than these shall he do, because I go unto My Father." - John 14:10-14.

God's transforming power and grace is changing my life from ordinary to extraordinary! As the Holy Spirit leads me to minister in God's anointing; I glorify His almighty name. The world is thirsting for the manifestation of the sons of God; and I'm humbled that He has appointed me for such a time as this!

Thank you Father for loving me so much, and for the rest of my life, by faith, I'm totally surrendered to His Kingdom service as a child of the Most High!

Praise God!

- March 28, 2012

"For verily I say unto you, That whosoever shall say unto this mountain, Be thou removed, and be thou cast into the sea; and shall not doubt in his heart, but shall believe that those things which he saith shall come to pass; he shall have whatsoever he saith."

- Mark 11:23

CHAPTER 16

SPEAK IT IN FAITH AND GOD WILL PROVIDE!

Last summer, August of 2011, I was diligently training for my third marathon! I was running and cross training at the health club; swimming three times a week. My training seemed to be on track and my dedication had elevated. It was during this time that my car's transmission went out and my previous work out partner had stopped providing a ride for me to get to the club. Satan was on the attack to discourage me from continuing my efforts to train diligently for the marathon. This particular morning, I got out of bed strong in faith, and I *confessed* that I was going to get a new way to get to the health club! I declared,

> *"Be anxious for nothing but in all things by prayer and supplication, with thanksgiving, make all your requests known to God."* —*Philippians 4:6.*

It was shortly thereafter that I received a phone call from another friend, Rita. Being aware of my transportation challenge, she informed me that she was going to the area near the health club and wanted to see if I would like to get a ride there. She said that she could drop me off to exercise while she conducted business, and after which she would come back to get me! I thought...God is good! I'd just confessed that I would get another way to the club and almost in that same hour ...an answer to my confessed prayer... a ride had shown up!.

> *"Therefore I say to you, whatever things you ask when you pray, believe that you receive them, and you will have them." –Mark 11:24.*

Rita picked me up and dropped me off at the health club. She allowed me the time I needed so I was able to complete my regimen of running and swimming. While in the pool, doing my laps, I noticed a new African American woman in the water aerobics class. I'd been going to this club for the last two years, and was now familiar with the members who regularly attended that class, and I knew that I'd never seen her before.

I finished my laps and headed to the shower. It was always my goal to get to the shower before the water aerobic class was dismissed, so that I would not have to wait for a stall. I had completed my shower and was drying off when this new Black woman walked in. She spoke to me and complimented me on my swimming cap; asking where I'd purchased it. I responded to her, telling her that a friend had bought it for me, but I could get her the information as to where it was purchased.

While speaking to her, the Holy Spirit, in His still small voice, started talking to me. He told me to ask her where she lived. Now... I'm standing there naked... drying off, and the Holy Spirit is telling me to ask this woman that I don't know, "Where do you live?" Being obedient to the spirit, I first asked her, her name. She told me that her name was Mary. I then asked her, following the directions of the Holy Spirit, "Mary, where do you live?" She being also naked and entering the shower replies that she lives in Maywood. The Holy Spirit persisted and prompted me to ask her to tell me exactly where. Now, I'm feeling a little awkward and uncomfortable to ask this additional question of this unfamiliar and very naked woman.

Even so, in obedience to the still small voice of the Holy Spirit that was speaking to me, I asked Mary, "Where in Maywood do you live?" She answered me, telling me that she lived on 2nd and Roosevelt! I chuckled inside for I knew where the Holy Spirit was taking this line of questioning. I told her that I would allow her to finish her shower, and would talk with her later in the locker room, and would share with her ...*why* I'd ask her those questions.

As I dressed, I was having a conversation with yet another club member inside the locker room. She jokingly reminded me of what I had told her a while back. She'd asked me if I'd gotten married... You see, I'd told this woman a few months earlier that I was getting married, and that God had released my husband and he was looking for me! As the conversation continued, Mary, now in the next set of lockers, overheard us talking and joined in by saying, *"He who finds a wife finds a good thing, and obtains favor from the Lord." –Proverbs 18:23* I was delighted in Mary's response; speaking the Word, confirming the Holy Spirit's instructions to me, to go over and talk with her. Now fully clothed, I approached Mary to finish our "Shower Stall" conversation.

I told Mary that I had been directed by God to speak with her and it was He... blaming it on The Holy Spirit...that had me, to ask her where she lived, and that I would now tell her why. I shared my story of working out at the club, and that I was training for a marathon. I went on to tell her that my car was not working and that I was in need of transportation.

At this point, I am fully persuaded by the Holy Spirit... that she was my *answered prayer!* So, I asked her if it would be alright to get a ride with her to the club whenever she would be coming. Mary answered me, confirming to me that she was new to the club, and was coming to the water aerobic class to rehab her shoulder. Today was her very first day in the class, and she would be coming every Monday, Wednesday and Friday. She responded with yes that I could ride with her, and that it would be no problem at all to pick me up. After all, the Holy Spirit had divinely positioned me to receive her help, making it very convenient as I lived right up the street on 9th and Roosevelt, in Maywood as well, only seven blocks away! Mary shared that she would be going to the health club on the very same days I'd gone for almost two years! Praise the great Omniscient ... all knowing God!

Additionally, the Holy Spirit intentionally selected Mary for me for other reasons!

As Mary and I continued talking, I knew by her spirit that I was talking with a woman of God. I asked her "Where do you worship?" She told me the name of her church, and I shared with her that I belonged to Living Word Christian Center. She replied that she had attended LWCC before as well. In fact, she had attended for some time while her church was experiencing leadership changes. It had been her family's church that she'd grown up in, and after the new leadership was in place she felt it was time to go back home, so she left LWCC. Mary did share that while at Living Word; having been directed by a co-worker to go there to find a church where she would be fed on the incorruptible Word of God, she had taken both the Foundation Classes and the Intercessory Prayer Classes!

I was too excited right about now... Look at how good God is! Not only had He provided me new transportation, but a new friend, equally yoked in the Word of God! My my my! God answers prayer...not often in the way in which you will expect it to come... but ...He does answer! *"According to your faith, be it done unto you!" -Matthew 9:29-30*

It's been about a year and Mary and I have become more than work out friends. She is truly a gift of God and we have become spiritual sisters of the Kingdom! Our time together has become a time of worship and devotion. In the car, we listen to CD's of God's Word as taught by Pastor Winston. Sometimes I bring other devotional readings that I share with her as she faithfully drives us to the club.

She has been such a blessing to me! In a time of need, God provided in her, more than I ever expected or even thought to ask for...

I thank the God that I serve, and call Father... for His faithfulness to me. He is my provider and I'm committed to walk by faith and not by sight. My natural circumstances on that morning were gloomy relative to transportation to the club, and in my natural strength, I was discouraged about the outlook of being able to maintain my cross training regime...

But confession steeped in unwavering faith... out of my mouth for a new way to get there; supernaturally invoked God's spiritual law with my tongue...

This story continues to confirm that what I speak in faith, without doubt in my heart ... God will provide! For He said in His Word, *"Death and life are in the power of the tongue and those who love it will eat its fruit."* —*Proverbs 18:21*

Praise God for His everyday miracles and the subtlety of He Himself; orchestrating the ordinary events in my life! The Holy Spirit speaks in a still small voice... while powerfully delivering the supernatural!

- March 30, 2012

"Now unto him that is able to do exceeding abundantly above all that we ask or think, according to the power that worketh in us,"
                                        - Ephesians 3:20

CHAPTER 17

AUTHORITY HALTS WORKPLACE ABUSE

Last year, summer of 2011, I received a call from my sister Danielle, who lives in Charlotte, North Carolina. She appeared to be in an anxious state and began to share with me a story of workplace abuse. That very morning she had received a verbal tongue lashing, which she'd endured from her very new manager. Danielle had only been on her job a very short time, approximately four months. She called me in angst, telling me of this brewing situation, which now had her worried. She told me that her new boss had just confronted her, out in the open in front of peers; without the dignity of a private reprehend. She explained to me what had taken place, which caused her much concern.

Her boss had come at her in anger; with a tone of condescension and verbally attacked her. She told Danielle that she was angry with her, accusing her falsely of offenses, as well as attempting to intimidate her with a threat of taking her before the *Big Boss* for a meeting... As Danielle continued to share this story of her hostile work environment; mostly from this one manager, I listened with the compassion of a *Big Sister.* I did not appreciate the inappropriate treatment that a leader in the workplace would unleash on a subordinate, having been in a leadership role many times over during my career. Even if Danielle was guilty of all she was being accused of, there still is a way that is appropriate in which to address policy in a private manner; leaving the accused with their dignity and their spirit intact. Danielle finished her story and I could tell that she was very worried about her manager's threat that loomed over her head; which was... to be brought before the *Big Boss.*

Though I listened initially as Danielle's big sister, I begin to hear a still small voice speaking to me that I recognized as the Holy Spirit. My spirit began to take over and transformed me from the "Big Sister" realm ... to the realm of a believer; fully vested in the delegated authority given to me by the almighty God!

In righteous indignation, I stopped Danielle by saying to her, "Danielle, wait just a minute!" "You do not have to take that!" "Your Supervisor was way out of line, and inappropriate as a manager to confront you that way." As I was speaking, the voice of the Holy Spirit began to *boldly* instruct me on what to say next!

I told Danielle that she did not have to accept that kind of abuse from anyone! I reminded her as a believer and a child of the Most High; she needed to take her Authority as a believer and declare some things. I stated to her that I was using my Authority and *"Calling things that be not as though they were!" Romans 4:17.* Hearing from the Holy Spirit, I informed her that I had two things to pronounce about this matter... "First, there was *not* going to be any meeting with the Big Boss, so she did not need to be concerned or anxious over that threat!" I let Danielle know that we were standing in agreement, in unwavering faith! With the confidence I have in the Lord, standing on His infallible Word, I John 4:4, *"Greater is He that is in her than he who is in the world."* I boldly declared, using my authority... the certain outcome as spoken in my spirit! I went on to tell her, "Not only would there *not* be a *"so–called"* meeting with the Big Boss, but your manager, who acted inappropriately and unbecoming of a leader in the workplace; will come back... and *apologize* to you!"

Now, when I told Danielle that, I was moving in the spirit, being instructed on what to say to her by the still small voice of the Holy Spirit. Even on hearing me boldly make those decrees; I don't think that Danielle was fully persuaded that the situation would play out like I said. Nor did I get... that she believed at that moment, that her boss would ever apologize to her, given the circumstances. Even so, she agreed to stay in faith and to release any worry or anxiety over the situation. Before getting off the phone call, I told her, to doubt not…and that she was going to call me with a victory report of those two things I decreed, within a few days.

"Whosoever shall say to this mountain, be thou removed, and be thou cast into the sea; and shall not doubt in his heart, but shall believe that those things which he saith shall come to pass, he shall have whatsoever he saith."
-Mark 11:23.

As the days passed by, I would ask Danielle, "Has your manager said anything about your meeting?"   She would answer me no, stating her manager had not said anything to her since that confrontation. She told me that her manager was giving her the silent treatment by just ignoring her; part of the intimidation tactic, she was using in her immature management style.

After about a week, I received a phone call from my sister. When she called, she had victorious news!

Her manager came to her and told her that she wanted to talk with her, *now in private*. She shared with Danielle in the meeting that she needed to review some policy information with her, among other things; which gave Danielle the impression that it was a directive from the *Big Boss.*   She went on to actually tell Danielle that she was sorry, and apologized for last week's confrontational episode and her inappropriate actions.   Additionally, the "so- called" meeting was *not* going to happen!   There wasn't even a mention of one and it was never spoken of again!

My my my…what a God we serve! A God that gave us dominion and delegated authority! In the heat of our battles as a believer, God has given all of us the measure of faith. Like David, even before his battle with Goliath began, we too can boldly declare our outcomes in the name of the Lord of hosts, being fully persuaded that we are backed by the almighty, omnipotent God!

> *"This day the LORD will deliver you into my hand, and I will strike you and take your head from you. And this day I will give the carcasses of the camp of the Philistines to the birds of the air and the wild beasts of the earth, that all the earth may know that there is a God in Israel."*   *- I Samuel 17:46*

Danielle's outcome was exactly what we had called for; being strong in faith…

Victory one: The threat of a meeting with the *Big Boss* did not happen, consequently, Danielle was not taken before the Big Boss at any time.

Victory two: Danielle's manager did apologize to her…just like I decreed! Praise God for He is faithful!

This is another testimony of faith, and demonstration of the awesome authority we have as believers! God has equipped us for battles, with full armor and spiritual weapons of war. When used with His incorruptible Word; we are divinely positioned to always triumph in Christ!

Thank God for Victory over Trials as we use our Authority ... as believers... commanding a halt to abuse ... stopping it in its tracks... in the workplace!

- April 1, 2012

"Finally, my brethren, be strong in the Lord, and in the power of his might.

Put on the whole armour of God, that ye may be able to stand against the wiles of the devil.

For we wrestle not against flesh and blood, but against principalities, against powers, against the rulers of the darkness of this world, against spiritual wickedness in high places.

Wherefore take unto you the whole armour of God, that ye may be able to withstand in the evil day, and having done all, to stand.

Stand therefore, having your loins girt about with truth, and having on the breastplate of righteousness;

And your feet shod with the preparation of the gospel of peace;

Above all, taking the shield of faith, wherewith ye shall be able to quench all the fiery darts of the wicked.

And take the helmet of salvation, and the sword of the Spirit, which is the word of God"

- Ephesians 6:10-17

CHAPTER 18

BELIEVER'S AUTHORITY BACKS POLICE OUT OF DRIVEWAY!

Early one evening, in the spring of 2011, I was sitting in the living room of my home, looking out the picture window on the sights of 9th Avenue, in Maywood, IL. It was a pretty day and I was enjoying the calm of the moment. My son, Bryan, had just left to rejoin his friend, a female, in the driveway. He had just come in for a bathroom break as he and his friend were headed out for the evening. He had only been downstairs about ten minutes when two police cars quickly arrived in front of the driveway, with the officers of each car, speedily dispatching from their cars as if answering a call for alarm!

My *natural* impulse was to become anxious as to their reason for arriving at my driveway and jumping out of their cars with such haste. My heart jumped a beat for just a moment when my *spiritual* being took over and started to dominate. I remembered my calming scripture on which

I've anchored my faith in uncertain times. *"Be anxious for nothing but in all things by prayer and supplication, with thanksgiving, make all your requests known to God."* -Philippians 4:6.

As I listened to the Holy Spirit, the still small voice inside; instructing me to begin speaking the Word, I remembered my *rights* as a believer… I begin to stand in my authority, as my phone that was already in my hand, begins to ring. It was my son calling. I answered the call in which he asked me to come downstairs. As I begin to walk toward the door, the Holy Spirit instructed me to stay calm while directing me to speak the Word. I quietly begin to speak ... *"Be anxious for nothing but in all things by prayer and supplication with thanksgiving, make all your requests known to God."* As I walk down the two flights of stairs, my believer's authority took over! I begin to proclaim and decree some things!

I started *"Calling things that be not as though they were."* - *Romans 4:17.* I declared, in the name of Jesus, that there would be no drugs found on my property! I decreed there would be no drugs found on Bryan or in his car. I proclaimed that Satan would not devour my son by his trickery, or that of police he often uses to do his dirty work! Last but not least, I decreed with the delegated authority given to me by God, that those police *must* back out of my driveway and get back in their cars, as swiftly as they had descended upon my property!

By the time I was at the bottom of the stairs, I was in full throttle authority… that I was performing in the spiritual realm. In the calm of moving in the spirit, I attempted to open the door to go out. The male officer ordered me to wait; holding the door closed as he was reviewing Bryan's driver license. Bryan was standing by his car, one leg still in the vehicle. Moments later, the officer allowed me to come out of the door onto the driveway.

When I asked the police, what was going on… Bryan responded saying, "Harassment is going on! They're just harassing me and I need to sue them for harassment!" At Bryan's reaction, the female officer; as she was physically … *backing out* of my driveway, spoke up… saying to Bryan, that he could take her badge number and try to sue her if he'd like…

With that being said, both officers quickly continued to literally *back off*, never responding to me at all… or to my question. They *swiftly* got in their cars and sped off!

Wow! They never said a word to me! Once I came out of the door being in spiritual authority, they responded to the supernatural command of the Holy Spirit which was directing me; *to back out of my driveway!*

When they had left as suddenly as they had come, I asked Bryan if he knew why they had come. He said that he didn't. I then asked him if they had searched his car or him. They had not… They had quickly come and as ordered; commanded in the spirit... They speedily left... seemingly coming for no reason at all!

I went back in the house as Bryan and his friend left to continue their evening. While back in the house, the Holy Spirit begins to speak to me. He wanted me to call Bryan and asked Him again, if he knew why those two police cars had been dispatched to my home. So I did...

When I asked Bryan did he have any idea on why they came, he told me that he didn't. By now the Holy Spirit had downloaded in me to share this with him. I told him that he may not know why the police came, *but I know why they left so suddenly*...

He asked me to tell him...

I told him the police officers left... and the reason that they backed off of the driveway so quickly; without searching him and/or his car, was because *I had ordered it!* Their speedy arrival and descent made no sense at all...to come with such force; two squad cars and two officers who rushed out as if looking for something... And then, *not* do any of the usual things that cops do... like search...

I knew that Bryan would not really grasp what I was saying nor would he know how the power of the Holy Spirit had *usurped* the plan of the police after they had arrived. Even so, the Holy Spirit wanted me to share this with him; to let him begin to see, and know the power and authority that is working in me as a believer.

As I continue to pray that God will show Bryan... His great salvation and save him... I stand in the gap for his Kingdom citizenship. Soon he will realize and come to know the power of the Holy Spirit and the spoken Word of God... to overrule things in this earth.

> *"The wicked watcheth the righteous, and seeketh to slay him. The Lord will not leave him in his hand, nor condemn him when he is judged." –Psalms 37:32-33*

That driveway scene was nothing short of the Supernatural protecting me, and my son.

> *"The seed of the righteous shall be delivered."*
> *–Proverbs 11:21*

> *"Greater is He that is in me than he that is in the World" –I John 4:4.*

-   April 1, 2012

"No weapon that is formed against thee shall prosper; and every tongue that shall rise against thee in judgment thou shalt condemn. This is the heritage of the servants of the Lord, and their righteousness is of me, saith the Lord."

- Isaiah 54:17

CHAPTER 19

BY HIS STRIPES I AM HEALED...
EXTRACTING TOOTH PAIN BY FAITH!

In July of 2011, my new tenant of four months, Sarah, was experiencing severe tooth pain. Her suffering went on for weeks, as she didn't have dental insurance. She was on a waiting list to be seen at the free dental clinic of Stroger's Hospital. During that time, I watched Sarah walk around throughout the day, still doing her chores, but holding her face because of the persistent pain. Inasmuch as she was taking *"over the counter"* pain relievers, she was not getting any lasting relief from pain, and on some days she seemed close to tears.

When I asked her about the delay in going to the dentist, she told me about the dental appointment that she had made. She had called Stroger's Hospital with a desperate request, to be seen as an emergency. Even so, the first appointment they could give her was still thirty days away, in August.

Sarah and I happen to be in the hallway at the same time late one afternoon. She shared with me what was going on... with this now toothache of endless weeks! Her normal sleep schedule had been interrupted as well as her awake hours were tormented because of the unrelenting pain...

I stood on the 2nd floor as we talked... a staircase apart. As she was speaking, I began to not only feel compassion for her suffering, but I begin to hear a still small voice; the voice of the Holy Spirit. The Holy Spirit was telling me to ask her if she wanted me to pray for her... I could clearly hear His voice, even so, I was resistant to ask Sarah what I was being instructed to do by the Holy Spirit. I was reasoning in my head...that she has known me less than four months, and would probably not want me, or anyone to pray for her... that she didn't know.

After a few minutes of exchanging my excuses with the instructions of the still small voice ...which I knew was the Holy Spirit, I was *compelled to be obedient.*

I asked Sarah if she wanted me to pray for her. Her immediate response was yes; without any hesitation...at all... I went down the flight of stairs to where she was standing. I placed my hand on her, and I told her that I was praying a prayer of faith for her healing.

I stood on scripture, *Romans 4:17, "Calling things that be not as though they were."* After I had finished praying, I told her by faith... Her healing was now... that her tooth pain was gone! I said to Sarah, regardless of what happens, and even if the pain returns… "To remain immoveable in her faith!" I reiterated that she should stay in faith by repeatedly declaring, *"By His Stripes I am healed" -Isaiah 53:5*

Sarah began to repeat the Scripture while walking away, and thanking me for prayer.

She told me a few days later that the pain was completely gone, and that she was continuing to stay in faith by speaking, *"By His stripes I am healed."*

In August, Sarah was still planning on keeping her much awaited dental appointment. She really wanted to have the tooth extracted; never to have pain from that tooth again. Unfortunately, Stroger's dental clinic, called and cancelled her appointment for reasons not known. Meanwhile, she was not having pain then, and had *not* had any more pain since the day of prayer.

Months later, during the winter …just before the Holidays, Sarah and I were talking. This is when she shared with me, that she had *Never* had her tooth extracted. I did not know this up until this point in time. She went on to tell me that the pain… *Never* came back! She had continued declaring her healing and saying in faith, *"By His stripes I am healed."*

Sarah told me how she had been sharing her story of miracle healing; her testimony of faith… with her family.

As she continues to share what happened in the stairway when I prayed for her, she is encouraging her family to pray and have faith as well. They now call her... to ask her how they should deal with illness and pain. Sarah, now having a personal story of faith and healing, continues to say to her family what I taught her to declare for her personal restoration. "Have faith in God and keep speaking and decreeing" ... *"By His stripes I am healed!"*

> *"A man's heart plans his way,   But the Lord directs his steps."* *—Proverbs 16:9*

- April 2, 2012

"Jesus saith unto them, My meat is to do the will of Him that sent me, and to finish His work."

- John 4:34

CHAPTER 20

SOW A SEED AND YOUR STOLEN
MONEY WILL BE RECOVERED!

On Mother's Day of 2012, I was sitting in church with my niece Misty and her daughter Alana, who were visiting Living Word Christian Center for the first time. I was excited to have Misty as a guest in my home church, as I had made several visits to her home church in Atlanta! Following a great Praise and Worship service, Pastor Winston gave a phenomenal seed message on the *Law of Sowing and Reaping.* As per usual, the time for giving of tithes and offering followed. As the ushers passed out the baskets for collecting, Misty leaned over and quietly spoke to me. She shared with me the unfortunate circumstances of her last evening while out with friends. Misty told me that while she was on the dance floor, someone had stolen $80.00 from her purse. Without a lot of lamenting with her, I immediately responded to the still small voice of the Holy Spirit as He instructed me on what to tell her. The Holy Spirit told me this, "Tell Misty to sow a seed and she will get her money back!" Without any hesitancy, I repeated what I'd heard from the voice of the Holy Spirit. I told Misty, "Sow a seed and you will get your money back!"

> *"Give, and it shall be given unto you; good measure, pressed down, and shaken together, and running over, shall men give into your bosom. For with the same measure that ye mete withal it shall be measured to you again." - Luke 6:38*

Pastor's sermon on "The Wealth Transfer" was awesome! After service, we were excited to head to our reservations for Mother's Day brunch at the beautiful Carlisle! I was really looking forward to gathering as a family this Mother's Day, and was delighted to be accompanied by Misty, Alana and Jessie; Misty's guest from Atlanta. In addition, Tresse, Reagan, and Sean, who had attended his own church, joined us later.

A couple of weeks prior to Mother's Day, I passed by the Carlisle and I saw the sign, advertising their upcoming brunch. My first reaction was that I'd love to go out for Mother's Day brunch; a tradition I enjoyed for many years with my Mom and sisters. Things had certainly changed in the last five years since Mom's passing, and I really longed for times shared, creating new memories and building on family tradition.

So, notwithstanding the price of brunch or how it may or may not fit into my budget of today; I planned the outing and made the reservation. I was totally in faith that Philippians 4:19 is true about my life! *"My God shall*

144

supply all my need according to His riches in glory in Christ!"

We had a great time eating and sampling more food choices than one could possibly imagine! From waffles to prime rib, it was all laid out for our culinary pleasure! After we were all filled and I must say a little stuffed, we shared our plans for after brunch. Some of us were headed in different directions; to share the rest of Mother's Day with other family members. I was going to the cemetery to honor the memory of my Mom on what was *still*, and always would be her day.

It was now time to pay up for the feast. Our waiter delivered the check and to our delight and surprise, Sean, the only man at the table, announced that He would be treating us all! Wow! We were thrilled to be treated so wonderfully, especially the mothers at the table which included Misty, Tresse and myself. Sean paid the check, tipped our waiter and we headed out of the Carlisle. We took time to take a few pictures out in front of this beautiful facility. Its white exterior beautifully decorated with its frontal gazebo, made a perfect backdrop for family memories captured in pictures!

The next day as I was sitting at my desk, I heard a familiar voice and quickly recognized it as the voice of the Holy Spirit. He said to me, "Call Misty and tell her she got her $80.00 back!"

Even though I'd missed it on Sunday, when it happened, I knew *immediately* what the Holy Spirit was saying to me now! I responded by texting Misty, even though she was at work. I wrote to her that I'd received a message from the Holy Spirit that He wanted me to give to her, and I asked her to call me. Only minutes later, Misty called. She asked me what was the meaning of my message. I asked her if she remembered what she told me on yesterday about someone stealing her money. She said that she did. I then asked her if she remembered what I told her, "Sow a seed and you will get your money back." She answered that she remembered. I then went on to tell her, *"And you got it back!"* She quickly responded saying in wonder, "From whom?" I answered her by saying, "From Sean!" It was an *"Ah Ha"* moment when she finally realized what had happened, and that she really did get her money back!

Misty exclaimed, "Oh, my God! You're right... I got the $80.00 back!" She realized that the money Sean covered, on what would have been her brunch tab, was exactly $80.00; the amount that was stolen from her! Faith in God to return a harvest for seed sown, delivered the exact results that had been prophesied only four hours earlier! Faith is now... and God is a *right now* God!

This was nothing short of the manifestation of the sons of God! The Holy Spirit's financial miracle for Misty within hours of it being called; continues to leave me in awe of His power! In addition to *demonstrating* the subtlety of the Supernatural, this also illustrates the power of the Kingdom's *Law of Sowing and Reaping*. When I told Misty to sow a seed and she would get her money back, she did! Her step of faith combined with the law of sowing and reaping resulted in an immediate harvest! Misty received back what Satan had unlawfully stolen!

God's awesome power continues to dominate in all ways and at all times! I praise Him for He is good...and He is good... all the time! I live my life in faith, unwavering in the infallibility of God's Word... and I *"Call things that be not as though they were!" – Romans 4:17.*

- June 12, 2012

"Give, And it shall be given unto you; good measure, pressed down, and Shaken together, And running over, Shall men give into your bosom. For with the same measure that ye mete Withal it shall be measured to you again."

- Luke 6:38

CHAPTER 21

THE SUBTLETY OF THE SUPERNATURAL... REAGAN'S CHILLS CEASE IN AN INSTANT

In May of 2012, my Granddaughter, Reagan who was six years old was experiencing an illness in her body that was causing her to have a fever. She had been sick for five days and her Mom had kept her home from school the entire week. It is important to mention here that over the last year or so, I had been teaching Reagan the scripture about divine healing and instructing her to speak it to her illnesses and discomforts; *"By His stripes I am healed." –Isaiah 53:5.* She has really grasped this verse and will say it when she is not feeling well, and when it seems as if she might be experiencing the symptoms of a cold. On hearing her repeat after me one day, "By His stripes, I am healed;" I decided to check with her on if she really understood what she was saying. I asked her, "When you say that, whose stripes are you talking about?" She looked at me and answered, "Grand Dee, I'm talking about God, by His stripes, I am healed!" Well praise the Lord! They will learn what they are taught! Glory be to God for sharing the Word with my Grand Daughter!

In caring for her during this particular episode of her not feeling well, I continued to tell her to repeatedly say, *"By His stripes I am healed."* On Thursday of that week, my nephew Sean came by my home. I told him about Reagan being there and for whatever reason, felt the need to explain. I said to him that she had been sick all week. With my *unconscious* mind, I told him that she *has* a urinary tract infection.

Reagan spent the night with me, staying out of school now the 5th day, while her Mother went to work early that morning. When I awaken the next day, the Holy Spirit smacked me in my face with His unquestionable voice asking, *"My daughter, does Reagan have a urinary tract infection or is she healed by My stripes?"* Oh my God! The Holy Spirit was bringing to my remembrance what I had spoken to Sean about Reagan. Inasmuch as had I told her all week that *she* should say, *"By His stripes I am healed,"* my words to Sean totally undermined what God was doing with her... by now granting power to an illness... giving it a name and a position in her body! I quickly apologized to the Holy Spirit and cancelled those words that I had unintentionally spoken over her, and standing on Isaiah 53:5, I again decreed that *"By His stripes she is healed!"*

Later that same morning; after being called on the carpet by the Holy Spirit, I was in my office working, when Reagan awaken and came in. She was shivering with chills and continued to have a fever. She spoke and said to me, "Grand Dee, I'm cold and I can't stop shaking!" Responding in a natural way to comfort her, I had her to lie down on the sofa and I covered her with a throw to warm her. She laid there for about ten minutes before saying to me,

"Grand Dee, I can't stop shaking and my teeth keep chattering!" As soon as she spoke this to me, the Holy Spirit downloaded in my spirit with His authoritative voice, saying to me, *"You know what to do!"*

In obedience to His voice, I responded by asking Reagan to come to me. I placed my hands on her and went into prayer, standing firmly in agreement with the Word of God and *"Calling things that be not as though they were,"* I commanded the shaking and chattering to stop!

In that exact moment, Reagan's chattering of her teeth and the shaking of her little body; *immediately* ceased! A great calm; reminiscent of when Jesus spoke to the sea and said *"Peace be still!"* took its place! The *miraculous stillness* was obvious to anyone who might have witnessed what had just happened; even so, to be clearly obvious to my then six year old Grand Daughter, was proof of the power of the Holy Spirit, that was *demonstrated!*

Reagan looked at me in amazement and in great awe she asked me, "Ooh... Grand Dee, how did you do that?" She was asking me how in the world did I make everything stop so suddenly... She knew the *"suddenness"* was not normal but extraordinary, not a thing that just happens!

I've often heard my Pastor say "Christianity was never meant to be dictated; but to be demonstrated. One act of manifestation of the sons of God is worth more than a thousand sermons!"

In that incredible moment of hearing from God and being obedient to His voice; my Grand Daughter was able to witness the amazing power and "The Subtlety of the Supernatural!"

I was totally being led by the Holy Spirit that morning! Staying available to the still small voice of the Spirit, and thirsting for communion with Him keeps me in position to receive His fellowship! Being awakened and admonished for my careless words and given the opportunity to ask for forgiveness; paved the way for me to set things right spiritually, so that I might later hear from God, in such a powerful way! It cleared the way for an awesome act of God!

I am in awe as I continue to experience the unlimited power of the Holy Spirit! I am humbly walking in dominion as I go about doing my Father's business! I expect the miraculous in my daily life, and I will continue standing on scripture,

"Verily, Verily, I say unto you, He that believeth on Me, the works that I do shall he do also; and greater works than these shall he do; because I go to my Father." —*John 14:12*

- June 12, 2012

"And such as do wickedly against the covenant shall he corrupt by flatteries: but the people that do know their God shall be strong, and do exploits."

- Daniel 11:32

"And Jesus said unto him, Go thy way; thy faith hath made thee whole. And immediately he received his sight, and followed Jesus in the way."

- Mark 10:52

CHAPTER 22

MY MIRACLE ENCOUNTER WITH THE HOLY SPIRIT AT THE LAUNDROMAT!

The Supernatural is ever-present in my life! The Holy Spirit is my Invisible Partner and His companionship abounds mightily in my every day! I am very excited to share this encounter and adventure with my *Ever Present Help!*

A couple of weeks ago, on August 16, 2013, I needed to go the Laundromat to wash a comforter. Before arriving in its parking lot, I thought for a minute, "I hope that I have the $7.00 in cash I need to exchange for quarters to pay for the wash cycle."

I parked my car and reached for my purse. I went into my wallet and counted one ten dollar bill, a five and two singles. So I quickly grabbed the five and two singles. I put my wallet back in my purse and put my purse on the floor of the car. I gathered the comforter and went into the Laundromat...leaving my purse in the car. As I went in, I stuffed the comforter in a washer and walked to the coin machine to exchange my $7.00 for quarters.

Before inserting my money into the changer, I emptied my right pocket of keys so that I might use the empty pocket as a receptacle for the coins, that I would need to carry back to the washer.

I then inserted my $7.00 into the money changer. I scooped my $7.00, now in coins, out of the money changer with my hand, and put them into the empty pocket on the right. I walked over to the washer with my pocket full of quarters and began depositing the money into the washer. When I'd put in $6.50, the washer began its cycle... I then took the remaining two quarters that I had left over, and I put them back into my right pocket... My *empty* right pocket...

Upon pulling my hand out of the pocket, I opened my hand and discovered the $7.00 was back in my hand!

I looked at the $7.00 saying, "Oh My God...Holy Spirit... I recognize You! I asked Him, what is going on?" I asked Him, "What are you saying to me?"

My natural mind quickly begin to question itself, asking if I had gotten the quarters from the change machine.

The Holy Spirit quickly answered, saying, "The machine is going!" That was easily confirmed as I stood in front of the washer with my comforter in it, as it was now in the wash cycle! My mind flashed; remembering the walk to the change machine...confirming that I indeed had exchanged the $7.00 for the coins. *I knew for sure that the Holy Spirit* *had supernaturally replaced the $7.00 that was now back in my hand!*

I went back to my car to get my purse and a bag that contained a book and writing materials. I came back into the Laundromat and instead of reading; the Holy Spirit prompted me to write a letter. I began writing and as I am writing, I wanted to insert a particular scripture into the text of the letter. I remembered that I'd placed my Blackberry in my purse, which I maintain as a convenient way to reference verses that I use in my prayer life. At first, I attempted to find my Blackberry without looking into my purse by just reaching into it and searching blindly its contents. After my blind search could not find it, I retrieved the purse and placed in on my lap. I then opened my purse so that I could peer inside. As I looked inside of my purse... to my amazement I discovered yet another $7.00!

By now I am fully convinced of the magnitude of the Holy Spirit's manifestation, and of His supernatural presence! I spoke out loud, *"Holy Spirit, what is going on? What are you telling me?"*

In that moment, *He immediately* downloaded in me this revelation... As He spoke to me in His unquestionable voice that seemed audible and loud enough for all to hear... *"Not only am I restoring and replenishing you; I am giving you double for your trouble!"*

There I was experiencing the Supernatural once again...signs...wonders and miracles! I'd come into the Laundromat with just $7.00, yet I now was in possession of two more $7.00, and a clean comforter! I went home filled with the joy and the magnificence of which I'd just witnessed... The visible power of the Holy Spirit, in *demonstration!*

Once I was home; the Holy Spirit began to give me more revelation knowledge on what I'd just experienced...

He reminded me that earlier that morning, I'd been listening to Pastor Winston's broadcast in which he was speaking on his series; "The Power of Confession." Pastor Winston explained that the Hebrew word for replenish and restore is *Chayah.* Pastor gave instruction to the viewing audience, He said, "Say, *Chayah* and touch your purse, touch your wallet!" Well, I thought that I would obey my prophet and do just what he was suggesting! I took that step of faith and ran and grabbed my purse and wallet, proclaiming... *"Chayah!"*

The Holy Spirit fully revealed to me, that my response this morning to Pastor's instruction... *initiated* a spiritual law! This spiritual law was it ignited and set in motion, first by me, *believing* in the Word of the Lord, and then *being obedient with an action of faith,* which produced the supernatural manifestation that replenished my $7.00 as quickly as I spent it... in multiples!

The Word says in, II Chronicles 20:20... *"Believe in the Lord your God, and you shall be established; believe His prophets, and you shall prosper."*

I feel honored and privileged to behold the supernatural virtue of the Omnipotent, Omnipresent and Omniscient God!

To be used as a vessel where the Holy Spirit moves powerfully in demonstration of signs and wonders; is mind boggling and life altering! I praise God that He chose *me* for such a time as this! He says in His Word...

> *"You did not choose Me, but I chose you and appointed you that you should go and bear fruit, and that your fruit should remain, that whatever you ask the Father in My name He may give you."*
> *– John 15:16*

The end time power of the church is ever increasing as we do the things that Jesus did; as it serves the agenda of the King! I am surrendered to His agenda and His irrevocable plan for my life! He gets all the glory for it is only on His authority that the Supernatural flows, making the impossible... *possible!*

> *"Verily, verily, I say unto you, He that believeth on Me, the works that I do shall he do also; and greater works than these shall he do; because I go to my Father." - John 14:12*

"Believe in the Lord your God, so shall ye be established; believe his prophets, so shall ye prosper."

- II Chronicles 20:20

"Before I formed thee in the belly I knew thee; and before thou camest forth out of the womb I sanctified thee, and I ordained thee a prophet unto the nations."

- Jeremiah 1:5

CHAPTER 23

TESTIMONIES REFLECT MY HERITAGE AND POWERFULLY POINT TO JESUS...

Every testimony is an act of God and a pointer to my heritage! I am a child of the Most High... Omnipotent, Omnipresent and Omniscient God! Every supernatural act that He empowers to flow through my earthly vessel... points back to my heritage in Christ. I am only who I am... In Him!

- Every miracle that I've experienced, points back to Him!

- He is the Father and my identity is in Him. Hallelujah for divine Rhema!

- I am a son of God!

- I am in His family... His bloodline and all His abilities run through my blood.

- He's made me a master craftsman operating in the supernatural realm... doing the things that He did! His Word tells me...

> *"Verily, verily, I say unto you, He that believeth on Me, the works that I do shall he do also; and greater works than these shall he do, because I go to my Father." – John 14:12*

I received such a revelation... such a Rhema Word on this... as I was spending time with Him, in devotion. All the miracles that He chose to flow through me... were always testimony to me... first and foremost ... that I have His DNA, that I am a peculiar people... that I by His grace... and His grace alone...was purified through a wilderness... not of my choosing... for such a time as this... when He would call me to demonstrate His amazing power!

His demonstrated power is for His purpose of drawing all men unto Him!

I am humbled and in awe that His very power flows though me! What a privilege and an honor to call Him Daddy... and to proclaim with all that I am... *Abba Father!*

"Ye have not chosen me, but I have chosen you, and ordained you, that ye should go and bring forth fruit, and that your fruit should remain: that whatsoever ye shall ask of the Father in my name, he may give it you."

- John 15:16

ABOUT THE AUTHOR

Minister Denise D. Campbell has been a media sales executive, personal brand and leadership coach, educator, author, realtor, and keynote speaker. She has spent her career creating brand awareness for clients' products and services with the goal of establishing market presence resulting in revenue. Denise has been a Director of Ad Sales for BET, a Sales Manager with Cox Broadcasting, ABC, Disney, Infinity Broadcasting, an Account Executive with the Tribune Company selling sports for the Chicago Cubs and the Chicago Bears, the Executive Director of Ad Sales for the Chicago Defender and the Associate Publisher of Who's Who in Black Chicago. As a graduate of the School of Ministry at Living Word Christian Center; Denise is now a *"Minister of the Gospel;"* diligently pursuing the unveiling of God's "Destiny Mandate" on her life!

Minister Denise's passion for ministry and leadership propels and fuels her life's mission, which is to be an internationally respected *"Visionary Agent of Change;"* in the pulpit and the marketplace!

"Calling Things" is inspired by the Supernatural manifestations of God! This book and the miracles therein have been foundational to Denise's launch into her ministry calling...

Denise lives her life with passion and a commitment to be led by the Holy Spirit! Her *"Faith"* and trust in *"The Wisdom of God*," biblical truths and timeless core values, while embracing the spirit of passing on "earned knowledge and understanding," instructs her to live a life of service to others. Denise honors her loving Dad, Ernest Jones, Jr., and her gracious Mom, Florence Jones; both now deceased, for being her most influential mentors and biggest fans.

Denise has a BA from the University of IL in Chicago, a M. Ed from the University of IL in Urbana-Champaign, a MA from Northwestern University in Evanston, and a Ministerial Training Diploma from Living Word Bible Training Center in Forest Park, IL. Minister Denise is a nine time Marathon finisher; having completed four full and five half-marathons, which she feels is symbolic of life's journey; destiny demanding diligence! Denise is a Chicago native, and is the daughter of parents, Ernest and Florence Jones. She has three brothers and two sisters, a son, Ryan, a granddaughter, Ryauna and two grandsons, Jahmere and Jordan. Denise lives a paradigm of being an

Ambassador of the Kingdom, as she embraces God as the head of her life; forever settled on His Word as her compass for living! Having responded to His call, initially revealed through a vision; the foundational scripture for Denise's ministry is, *"Verily, verily, I say unto you, He that believeth on Me, the works that I do shall he do also; and greater works than these shall he do; because I go to my Father."*

- John 14:12